COURAGE & FAITH

the early years of o.c.s.c./cadence international

Courage & Faith: The Early Years of O.C.S.C./Cadence International

compiled and edited by Joyce Schroeder

designed by Lauren Reavely

CADENCE
PRESS

FOREWORD

The pages of the story of
OCSC/Cadence International have turned for
more than 60 years now. It is a story of the faithfulness of
God and the faithfulness of God's people. It is the story of courageous
missionaries, generous prayer warriors, and dedicated military people in and
through whom God has done mighty works.

As editor of this glimpse into the history of Cadence, I offer it not only as the wife of David
Schroeder, president of Cadence, but also as the daughter of Dick and Margaret Patty, who, along
with the Millers, the Tarkingtons, and the Hashes, were the founders of OCSC/Cadence International.
I grew up in military ministry and have spent my adult life in this ministry.

I tell you this because I want you to know that I have watched these people my entire life − that's 55 years at
the time of this printing! And I want you to know, these people are the real deal. They have authentically walked
with God. They have stepped out in faith; they have been life-long students of the Bible; they have endured deep
trials and suffering; and they have gone the distance in obedience to Christ. The three founders who are already in
heaven finished well. And those still living, now in their eighties, are still growing in faith and still trusting God.

The reason I believe these people are the real deal is because their trust is in Jesus Christ. And Jesus is the real
deal. He is the Way, the Truth, and the Life.

Psalm 44:1 says, "We have heard with our ears, O God; our fathers have told us what you did in their
days, in days long ago." These pages are the telling and showing of some of what God did in the early
days of Cadence. They are not comprehensive or exhaustive, but rather representative of the early
years of this ministry to military. My prayer is that they encourage and inspire you to walk with
God in your story, and to carry on the legacy of faithfulness modeled by the godly people
whose faces you see in these pages.

May Christ be exalted in the nations through the lives of
transformed military people,

Joyce Schroeder

THE BEGINNINGS

THE PIONEERING

THE EXPANSION

THE BEGINNINGS

1942-1954

THE FOUNDERS

*the faces and stories of the four couples who stepped out in courage and faith
to share the gospel and their lives with the military community*

BY CAROL HENDRY AND JOYCE SCHROEDER

Sid Hendry and O.C.S.C. founders at a board meeting

JOHN, JESSE, JUDY, JIM, NETTIE MILLER

JESSE & NETTIE MILLER

As a young soldier in the Philippines, Jesse grew in his faith under the ministry of missionaries Dad (Cyril) and Mom (Anna) Brooks. During this time he prayed, "Lord, if I ever have a home of my own, You can have it for servicemen" (*Prisoner of Hope*, 24). God honored this prayer – beyond what Jesse could then imagine. But before that, there was great suffering.

War broke out and Jesse was taken as a POW. He clung to the promises in Scripture he had memorized around the Brooks' dinner table as he survived the Bataan Death March and shared Christ with fellow prisoners.

Seven years after Jesse's release, servicemen gathered in Jesse and Nettie's home in the Philippines. God greatly used the Millers' strength of spirit, hospitality and Bible teaching.

In 1954, Jesse gathered Dick Patty, C.P. Tarkington, and Tom Hash to form Overseas Christian Servicemen's Centers. In his book Jesse wrote, "With many avenues of service open for a ministry among military, we joined in prayer that God would call and lead many who would obey His call and follow His leading, eager to serve in this ministry. We requested of God that a chain of centers would be established around the world" (171).

(L-R) DANNY, DOTTY,
DAVID, LORI, AND TOM HASH

TOM & DOTTY HASH

Dotty's hands flew up and down the piano keyboard as Tom's tenor led the packed crowd of servicemen, all on their feet, heartily singing, "Oh, victory in Jesus! My Savior forever!" Later in their living room and kitchen, Tom and Dotty fed soldiers who were far from home, filling stomachs with home cooking and hearts with Jesus' love.

While single, Tom followed the Lord as his Savior because of Jesse's ministry to him; then, as newlyweds, Tom and Dotty followed God's leading to minister to the military, first at the headquarters, then to Panama and beyond.

The lean times deepened their trust in God's faithful provision. Tom once wrote: "Today as I thought through the need for equipment, for passage, and for support, my heart was completely filled with the thought that Dotty's and my only real need is to be filled with the Lord. We are trusting the Lord to do this – that only He might be seen in these weak lives" (*Fill These Rooms*, 79).

In harmony with Jesus, Tom and Dotty actively practiced trust, always claiming victory in Jesus.

TOP PICTURE: TARK AND ALMA AT THEIR WEDDING
LOWER PICTURE: (L-R) ALMA, JO CAROL, TIMOTHY, TARK, LENA BETH
TARKINGTON

C.P. & ALMA TARKINGTON

Anyone privileged to be part of the ministry of C.P. "Tark" and Alma Tarkington would not soon forget their broad smiles and vibrant faith. Servicemen were welcomed by Tark's big handshake and booming drawl and Alma's sweet strength.

Like the other founders and the missionaries who have followed, Tark and Alma relied on God and His people to provide their income. Once, after securing a house to use for the ministry, Tark and Alma realized that the rent would take all their funds. Trusting in God's direction and provision, they paid it.

A week later, Officer Marshall walked into Tark's office. Tark had led him to the Lord earlier, and now this young, growing Christian felt the Lord was telling him to tithe. He said, "I've never given anything to anybody!" as he handed Tark a check for $200.

After serving in the Philippines, Tark and Alma pioneered the Cadence ministry on Okinawa. During their first term there they saw God build the Christian Center debt free, and it was dedicated in 1964. The Lord fully, faithfully provided.

MARGARET, STEVEN, JOYCE, DICK, AND DAVID PATTY

DICK & MARGARET PATTY

Taking the man out of the farm but not the farm out of the man, God used Dick Patty to plant and pioneer many ministries to the military. While establishing the Subic Bay Servicemen's Center, he proposed to Margaret on a tape. Margaret worked her way to the Philippines on a freighter, and they were married at the Manila Servicemen's Home. Immediately after returning from their honeymoon, they welcomed sailors into their home.

Dad Brooks advised them to take a night off: "It may be better to burn out than to rust out, but it's best to last out." Thus, after a couple years, they told the sailors that Monday night would be the Pattys' night off. The next Monday, more sailors showed up to the Center than usual. They were there to spend the evening off with Dick and Margaret.

Dick recently reflected, "We've outlasted some of the ministries we started." He was referring to the Subic Center and Switzerland Bible conferences. However, the youth ministry of OCSC/Cadence, grown from their home in Germany, continues to reach military dependents to this day.

The legacy of faithful obedience and loving service continues in countless lives touched by the wisdom, courage, and kindness of the Pattys.

(L-R) TOM HASH, CHUCK HALL, BILL PLEINS, AND C.P. TARKINGTON ON A "GOSPEL BOMB" RUN

BEGINNINGS OF O.C.S.C./CADENCE

by C. P. Tarkington in 1955

[Editor's note: The paragraphs in italics are the words of Jesse Miller.]

"We were defeated soldiers already, and the war had only started. On the Bataan peninsula we were placed on very meager rations. Soon my body began to swell. Ulcers were then coming out on my flesh. The same kind of sores that I had seen on those Filipinos that first day after arriving in the Islands. I came to realize then that it wasn't their fault. They needed more food — something Americans had plenty of. I love those souls now. I want to tell them of the Love of Christ, who is the Bread of Life, and the One who can stop their spiritual ulcers. The same Christ who walked with me on Bataan Peninsula, and all the way out of that Peninsula on the Death March.

It was my lot to teach the Bible class that evening to fellows who were filled with hatred and to men who had seen more than their share of death, disease, and starvation. It seemed like everything had been passed out to us since that horrible day: December Seventh. That was the day the Japanese seemed to wipe away all decency, spreading malice, hate, death and famine. It seemed to take deeper root with each onslaught of the enemy. Then came this night. The summit. This evening, in prayer, I opened my Bible and we listened to words beautifully spoken by Jesus: 'As Moses lifted up the serpent in the wilderness, even so must the Son of Man be lifted up. Look unto me and be ye saved all the ends of the earth: For I am God.'

There were nine men there that evening that knew not Christ. They all looked up into that wounded side and said, 'I know that Thou art God. I've seen enough sin and I want to be saved from it. Save me for Jesus' sake.' Those nine men were saved that night — the night before Bataan fell into Japanese hands, and the next day all of us stepped out on the Death March."

Eight years later, Jesse Miller, whose testimony is partially given in the foregoing paragraphs, was teaching another Bible class of servicemen in the U.S. Military Port of Manila. He had spent three-and-a-half years as a prisoner of the Japanese. God marvelously preserved his life during those tortuous years. Then, upon liberation, he entered Bible School in preparation for missionary service, and upon graduation, he returned to the Philippine Islands as a missionary.

TOM AND TARK AT JESSE AND NETTIE MILLER'S TABLE IN MANILA

This Bible class, eight years after Bataan fell was a bit smaller. There were only four fellows now. Only one of these knew Christ as his personal Savior, while the other three, Tom, Bill and I, Tark, were without the love of Christ in our hearts. In the faithful and patient ministry of the Word, and by living testimony, we three soon found Christ as our own.

Almost ten thousand miles from home, as new creatures in Christ, we followed the natural course of most young Christians, by clinging to those who were our spiritual parents in the Lord. In the small over-crowded apartment of the Millers, we would gather for Christian fellowship. They opened their home to us, and hospitality flowed from the doors. The Lord added to our little group other servicemen who came to know Him, as well as giving us the fellowship of a few sailors who were based across from us at Sangley Point. And so it was only three months after the first were saved, that God had enlarged our group to number some eighteen Christians.

As a growth from our fellowship in the Millers' home,

the G.I. Gospel Hour began. We alternated our services: one Saturday night at the Air Force Base in Manila, and the following week at the Naval Base in Sangley Point. This G.I. Gospel Hour gave each of us servicemen an opportunity to work, since the service was completely handled by servicemen. We invited a missionary speaker for each service, however. Through this means, other men were contacted for the Lord, and the group of Christians enlarged.

Even as the group grew, we continued to gather at the Millers' for fellowship. This little apartment became our "home away from home." Only the years of eternity will reveal the fellowship and the joy that was shared by homesick boys in the service of their country, as they met in this home away from home. And God alone knows how many came to know Him personally in that Home, and how many of us dedicated our lives to the Lord for His service while we were fellowshipping in that Christian Servicemen's Home.

After several months, it became quite evident that a larger place was needed. The Millers, and we G.I.s prayed about this. God had evidently called Jesse Miller and his wife to work among us servicemen. Their mission board graciously freed them from other responsibilities so that they could give their full time to work among G.I.s.

Then, in faith, believing God to supply all needs, we rented the first Christian Servicemen's Home in Manila. Every need was placed into God's hands, with no established stateside organization backing us. God be praised for the supplying of rent and food for every day and for every month.

With a radiant testimony on the lips of Christian G.I.s and with the evangelistic services of the G.I. Gospel Hour, the continuation of the Bible classes on the bases, and the evident change in fellows' lives who came to the Lord, other young men soon joined the group. Before another year passed it was necessary again to trust the Lord for a larger "Home." God worked miracles, and that home was provided in November of 1952, and is in operation today, with the "Christian Servicemen's Home" written over the door and welcoming any who enter.

In the fall of 1953, the Millers sailed home for a much needed furlough. God had provided another missionary couple, Mr. and Mrs. C. Nieuwsma to take charge of the work. Mr. Nieuwsma had also been a G.I. and understands the needs of servicemen.

When the Millers arrived in the States there were many requests from G.I.s who had been with them in the Philippines, that a conference or reunion be planned. In June, 1954, a group of us met in the Chicago China Inland Mission Home, which had been graciously lent to us for this purpose. Our time of fellowship in the Word of God is never to be forgotten.

During our meetings at this reunion, requests were presented to our group from the Philippines, Okinawa, Guam, Alaska, Germany and Japan to open up Servicemen's Homes such as God has given us in the Philippines. These requests were heavy on our hearts and brought us to our knees before the Lord. It was very evident that God was working in our hearts, and we were willing to do what He wanted us to do. Under God's leading, the Overseas Christian Servicemen's Centers was formed, to work and to represent Christ wherever God should lead, placing our faith in Him completely, and trusting Him to supply each need.

The Millers, at the time of this printing, plan to leave for Okinawa this fall *[editor's note: the Millers returned to the Philippines instead]*. Dick Patty, who found the Lord in a Servicemen's Center in Chicago in 1945 at the time he was serving in the Navy, is looking forward to going to Olongapo, Philippines, to work among the sailors there. We ask you to pray for more workers. My wife and I have one more year to finish school, and then we pray that God will send us out also to work among servicemen and to witness for Christ so that other servicemen may find Him, even as I did, in a "home away from home."

WHY SERVICEMEN'S CENTERS?

by Dick Patty

The Centers provide an atmosphere that is friendly to the moral and spiritual qualities which we desire to develop in the Christian life. Many a serviceman finds himself immersed in an atmosphere hostile to what is clean, noble, and spiritual. After awhile his sense of values begins to erode. The purpose of the Christian Service Center is not to encourage a man to escape from the hard realities of military life, but to help equip him to be a man of moral and spiritual integrity, able to draw upon the resources of God for better performance at his job.

Hours spent at the Center give a beleaguered Christian a chance to get his bearings again. The unsaved receive witness of the reality and value of the Christian life. Truths taught from God's Word are more easily embraced in an atmosphere that strongly supports their validity and significance.

Christian educators emphasize the importance of ministering to the "total man." The Christian Centers provide a choice setting for this. Some Centers serve over 600 meals a month, not because these men are suffering from malnutrition, but because the dinner table is a focal point of family living. When they are "home" at meal time, they are welcome at the table. The recreation, sing-spirations, trips, and hours of visiting meet physical, social, and emotional needs with a primary goal of ministering to spiritual needs.

(L-R) DICK, MARGARET, ALMA, NETTIE, TARK, AND JESSE

(BACK) BILL POWELL,
DICK PATTY,
AND JESSE MILLER
(FRONT) C.P. TARKINGTON,
BOB STOUT,
AND TOM HASH

CADENCE INTERNATIONAL

SHARING THE GOSPEL AND OUR LIVES WITH
THE MILITARY COMMUNITY.

CADENCE MISSION

EXALTING CHRIST IN THE NATIONS THROUGH
THE LIVES OF TRANSFORMED MILITARY PEOPLE.

CADENCE VISION

WE BELIEVE...

- *sacrificially serving the military community is a privilege.*
- *people in the military community need to know Christ.*
- *in the power of incarnate ministry.*
- *maturity is the fruit of engaging in a relationship with the Word of God, the Spirit of God, and the people of God.*
- *in equipping believers for Great Commission multiplication.*
- *in the responsible and strategic deployment of all God-given resources.*
- *teamwork maximizes ministry effectiveness.*

CADENCE CORE VALUES

NINE MUST DIE!

BY JESSE MILLER
AN EXCERPT FROM *PRISONER OF HOPE*

"THE LONGING TO BE WITH
CHRIST WAS VERY STRONG. I KNEW
THAT WOULD BE FAR BETTER FOR ME.
BUT WHAT ABOUT THE OTHER EIGHT
MEN WHO STOOD IN LINE WITH ME?
WERE THEY READY TO DIE?"

First Squad – All Present
Second Squad – All Present
Third Squad – All Present

Our nerves were tense. Why did this have to happen? Had one man really taken off? "Oh, God, be merciful. If possible please put a little love in the hearts of these guards."

Fourth Squad – All Present

As the bongo (roll call) progressed my heart pounded fearfully. I knew the penalty we would pay if one man was missing – death for all the rest of us in our ten-man squad. We had been forced to watch many of our comrades die on that horrible death march from the tip of Bataan Peninsula to Camp O'Donnell. We had been sternly warned that any attempt to escape would result in immediate death. We were weak from lack of food and disease was prevalent. The fact is that too many died without making an attempt to escape.

From Camp O'Donnell many of us were marched off to prison camp in Cabanatuan. All of it was enclosed by an eight-foot-high barbed wire fence, interspersed with frequent guard houses from which the enemy kept an eagle eye on us. I noticed that a certain area had three rows on these tall fences. Even so, due to severe mistreatment some prisoners tried to escape. Every prisoner was assigned to a ten-man group. My barracks housed a hundred prisoners, so there were ten squads in our barracks. If one escaped, the remaining nine would be lined up to face the enemy's rifles. With great apprehension we waited for the order for Squad Nine to report.

Fifth, Sixth, Seventh Squads – All Present

The roll call came closer. The finger of death was pointed at us. "Oh God, not us! Not me!"

Eight Squad – All Present
Ninth Squad – One man missing!

Suddenly my heart was quieted. I experienced the "peace of God which passes all understanding." It seemed strange to have peace and joy mixed in with tragedy. I knew I had eternal life through my faith in Christ Jesus. No man could take that assurance from me. Just a year before enlisting in the Army Air Corps, I had placed my faith in the salvation the Lord Jesus Christ had provided. I believed that His death took the penalty of my sin. Words of assurance were great comfort to me, "He who hears My Word and believes on Him Who sent Me, has everlasting Life and shall not come into condemnation but is passed from death into Life." (John 5:24) A deep and meaningful "Thank you, Lord" escaped my lips.

> *"IT IS BECAUSE OF THE LORD'S MERCIES THAT WE ARE NOT CONSUMED, BECAUSE HIS COMPASSIONS FAIL NOT. THEY ARE NEW EVERY MORNING; GREAT IS HIS FAITHFULNESS."*
>
> LAMENTATIONS 3:22-23

I knew I was facing death at any moment. I wondered how the others in my squad were facing the same prospect. Did they know the peace which comes from receiving forgiveness and acceptance as a child of God? (John 1:12)

Countless thoughts raced through my mind. I remembered Joe who died the first day the war reached us at Clark Field. Earlier in our friendship he had told me of his longing for something more in life. He shared with me that this desire began when his sister explained in her letter that she had placed her faith in Christ as her personal Savior and that joy and peace now filled her life. In all sincerity, Joe had asked me, "What can I do to be more fulfilled in my life?"

Rings of fresh dirt showed on his trousers when we walked back to our barracks. In the days that followed, Joe and I often met on a nearby hillside to pray and read and talk about God. Then suddenly it was December 8th! Clark Field was heavily bombed. The ambulance Joe was driving received a direct hit. Joe was taken from me.

The memory of Fred also flooded my thoughts. On the day war first reached us at Clark Field, we were a bunch of frightened young recruits, unprepared for war. In the midst of falling bombs, Fred, another buddy of mine, placed his faith in Christ. In the days of uncertainty, frustration, and suffering which followed, peace controlled him. His panic was gone. He no longer carried the guilt of sins. This brought a strong bond between us. Even though we became prisoners, we sensed a freedom in Christ. Three months later, both Fred and I were among the 60,000 prisoners who were forced to step out on the infamous Death March from Bataan. Physical life ended for Fred when he dropped from exhaustion and received the dreaded "cold steel process" from the enemy's bayonets.

Now as I was facing death, I thought I would soon be joining Joe and Fred. The longing to be with Christ was very strong. I knew that would be far better for me. But what about the other eight men who stood in line with me? Were they ready to die? At that strategic moment, I knew God was asking me if I was willing to tell each of them of Christ's salvation available to them.

"Oh yes, Lord, I am willing to do that and to go wherever You lead me, even back here to the Philippines or to the land of Japan." I meant that with all my heart.

Immediately, I knew there would be no massacre. As determined as our captors were to squeeze the triggers, they could not. It was God who intervened. The enemy officer commanded us to return to our barracks and ordered us to be prepared for the shooting the next morning. That evening I witnessed personally to every man in squad nine of Christ's substitutionary death for them. Each man was left with his own thoughts.

The next morning, there was no firing line to face. We were ordered back to work; most of us went back to slave labor in the fields and others to their work on airfield construction for the enemy. As I thought of the miracle that had taken place, I realized God's merciful care over me – He had kept me from a bomb hit; He had supplied strength to finish the Death March; I had not starved nor succumbed to severe fevers. Repeatedly, my life had been spared. Why? What purpose did God have for me? Again, I resolved I would follow Him wherever He would lead.

Three-and-a-half years later, at war's end, Jesse Miller arrived home safely. After completing his studies at Biola (Bible Institute of Los Angeles) he returned to the Philippines as a missionary with SEND International from where God led him and his wife into a life-long ministry focused on military service personnel.

ON FEBRUARY 22, 2001, JESSE MILLER PASSED TO HIS ETERNAL REWARD, "WITH THE LORD, WHICH IS FAR BETTER . . . TO AN INHERITANCE INCORRUPTIBLE AND UNDEFILED THAT FADETH NOT AWAY, RESERVED IN HEAVEN FOR HIM." (FROM PHILIPPIANS 1:23 AND 1 PETER 1:4)

THE
PIONEERING

1955-1959

THE PHILIPPINES

Our First Home

BY JESSE MILLER, FROM *PRISONER OF HOPE*

Nettie and I shared one of the Quonset buildings with the Honeywell family of five. They had the front two-thirds and we had the back one-third. I estimate our allotted space was approximately 20' x 20'. We shared a bathroom with the Honeywells.

The walls were single siding, with the two-by-fours inside. We covered these with plyboard, and divided the space into a tiny bedroom, kitchen and living-dining room. A room divider and a closet, which I built, separated these areas. The kitchen was Nettie's domain and she made it as home-like as possible with the very little she had available. I had my part in building the kitchen cupboards.

Our windows were of non-transparent celutex. Of course we kept them open most of the time in order to benefit from any breeze that came.

Eventually I built wood louver insets to replace the celutex. These provided better opportunity for air circulation and also a degree of privacy. Only those who have lived in the tropics can understand how hot and humid it is all the time. We had no air conditioning.

The roof over us was galvanized tin. A bamboo tree stood behind our place and its branches swung over the roof. At night we often heard rats climbing the tree and taking a jump onto the roof. They had great fun.

We were happy and content in that first home the Lord gave us, and today we enjoy wonderful memories of living there.

Now that I had a home of my own I remembered my promise to open my home to military people.

P.O. Box 1956

As the summer is now
quite spent, the Christian Servicemen's
home in Manila is completing its fifth year in exis-
tence. The foundation for the home – the Christian G.I.s themselves – has been laid for six years. Except for a brief furlough to the
States, Jesse has been directing this home and has been responsible for all its
outlets. In '52 when the Manila post office box number 1956 was first acquired,
the fellows used to say, "I wonder what the home will be like in the year 1956, and
what progress will be made?"

Now it is 1956, and the home's record is a blessed one, for countless men have either found
the Lord as their Savior through its ministry, or have gone through a deepening experience
in the Lord, never to be forgotten.

Sometime this fall, the home is to enter into a completely new phase, for it is to have a
new permanent director. C.P. Tarkington and his wife, Alma, along with their little boy,
Timothy, are expecting to be the new father and mother. And this home, that has
been so fruitful, is now sending the original director on to tasks of establishing
other homes.

Pray for this place of service as it looks forward to the next
instrument God plans to use there.

– O.C.S.C. BULLETIN, AUGUST 1956

CAVITE CITY & CONFERENCES

BY C.P. TARKINGTON

When Alma and I relieved Jesse and Nettie at the Manila Center in 1956, we were working with airmen for the military port area and sailors from Sangley Point. In 1957, the Manila Port Area was closed so we decided to move the ministry to Cavite City to be near the sailors at Sangley Point Naval Base.

We rented a small compound that had two houses. A small one-story house was a two-bedroom that we used for our family, and the other was a two-story building that we used for the Center. With two buildings we still did not have near as much room as we did in the large home in Manila.

It was during our days at Sangley that our two daughters were born. Also in that time we had the joy of discipling Buddy Schofield and Lou Harrison and joining Sid in traveling to Clark and leading Bible classes at the home of Sgt. Allen. There we met Ralph Porter, and Sid led him to the Lord. It was from this group that Chuck Hall began the Clark Center.

The Manila home was large enough that the Millers held Bible Conferences there. That was impossible in our Cavite facilities, which were much smaller even with two buildings. With our group combined with the Pattys' group from the Subic Center, we had to find a new location to hold the Bible Conferences. Dick and I got our heads together and found we could use Camp John Hay, the military rest center in the mountains of Baguio.

The conferences became a highlight. Twice a year our groups got together for fellowship and edification. For some, it was their time of salvation. We had great music, wonderful Bible teaching, small group discussions, afternoons of sports and relaxation, plus fun on the skit night. Everyone tried to get leave for the conferences, as it was a chance to get away from the tropical heat and spend five days in the cool mountain air and be spiritually fed.

We had great teachers in the missionary community who would speak at the conferences like Dad Brooks, Ed Spahr, Sandy Sutherland and Ray Frame, to mention a few. By the time Chuck Hall opened Clark Center and his group joined, it was decided by our Advisory Board that one of the three Bible teachers at the conferences should be one of the OCSC missionaries. I well remember that I was asked to speak in one of my last conferences. I was to teach the book of 2 Timothy, and I was so nervous I prepared for months in order to teach along with those "Missionary Giants."

I now have degrees from three wonderful Christian Colleges, but in none of these have I had any better teachers that the veteran missionaries in the Philippines who led our conferences.

Top image: *The two Cavite Center buildings in 1958*
Left: *Buddy Schofield*
Right: *Timothy (Lance) Tarkington helping a sailor with the Cavite Center sign*
Below: *Enjoying skit time at conference*

UPPER: TARK AND DICK AT BAGUIO CONFERENCE WITH SPEAKER BILL ORVIN ON RIGHT. BUD SHAFFER ON LEFT WITH BIBLE
LOWER: (L-R) CHUCK HALL, BEN CADY, JESSE MILLER, ANNA BROOKS, CYRIL (DAD) BROOKS, SID HENDRY, DICK PATTY

In July 1960, my husband and I were sent to a base overseas. We were real unhappy about this. But through our new neighbor, who was a Christian, we began to attend activities at the Christian Servicemen's Center. It was through faithful witnessing and words that we trusted the Word of God and are now members of God's family. We are surprised to see how much we are learning. We received a special blessing at the Bible conference, for it was there that we yielded our lives and all our earthly possessions to God. We have never known such peace and joy as we now experience in the Lord.

FROM NANCY, A SERVICEMAN'S WIFE

A little bamboo hut on Cubi Point in the Philippines could be called the birth place of the Subic Service Center. It was known as the "prayer tent" by the group of Christian Seabees who had built it at the edge of their tent camp for a place to meet together for Christian fellowship and Bible study. These men, on their seasonal rotation to C.B. Center, Port Hueneme, spent considerable time at the Oxnard Service Center in California and shared with Dick Patty, the director there, the burden they had for a Service Center in Olongapo.

In February of 1955, Dick joined sixteen fellows in Cubi Point to labor with them in bringing to reality the vision they had held for many months. They had no money, no equipment, no building, but great confidence in God's purpose and faithfulness to bless and use them.

Jesse and Nettie Miller and their son, Jim, along with Dick Patty on the S.S. Old Colony Mariner enroute from San Francisco to Manila, January 1955

The ship pulled out of San Francisco Bay waters early on the morning of March 8th. This was a special voyage for the S.S. Washington, for on her was the Lord's servant, Sid Hendry. Sid was welcomed joyfully in the Philippines. The Lord answered prayer in preparing the way for clearing of customs, immigration, etc. Sid is now settled and working with the Pattys. Every indication is that God sent him there. He finds the constant heat and humidity a trial, as it is for all missionaries, and needs prayer for sustained health. Sid is burdened as he sees the need among the men. He expresses it thus: "With all the information I had about existing conditions, the actual needs far exceed anything I had pictured. I pray God to use me effectively among these men."

– O.C.S.C. BULLETIN 1959

INTER-OFFICE COMMUNICATION

To MARGARET OLSEN   DATE MAY 10, 1955

FROM   THE STAFF

SUBJECT: ENGAGEMENT

MAGGIE OLSEN CAME IN JUST BEAMING WITH JOY
FROM A LONG DISTANCE CALL FROM DICK PATTY, HER BOY
A BEAUTIFUL RING
HER ROOMMATE DID BRING
A GIFT FROM MANILLA. THAY GUY IS SURE COY.

A LOVE STORY

as told by Margaret & Dick Patty

On my birthday in 1955, I was sleepily brushing my teeth very early when I was called to the phone. The girls in the Nav home were all up, expecting the call, and ready to get the ring from Dick out of the refrigerator where they'd hidden it. When I realized it was Dick on the phone, I dashed into our little front room and closed the door. My roommate pushed the door open and finally thrust a little box into my hand. I'd not expected a ring, and I was quite speechless, much to Dick's consternation! (What can you say in three minutes?)

Some time later a sense of fear gripped me! I was going 7,000 miles away to marry a man I hardly knew. I believed God had been leading us together, but I wrote Dick and expressed my desire to have Him show us again, one more time! He started a letter back, just a short paragraph, basically saying that he too would like another confirmation from the Lord. He laid the letter aside and continued to write after his devotions that day.

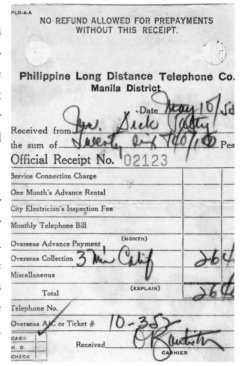

What God gave him completely dispelled my fears, and I've never doubted His plan again. It was I Chronicles 17:25-27 KJV, "For thou, O my God, hast told thy servant that thou wilt build him a house; therefore thy servant hath found in his heart to pray before thee. And now, Lord, thou art God, and hast promised this goodness unto thy servant. Now therefore let it please thee to bless the house of thy servant, that it may be before thee for ever. For thou blessest, O Lord, and it shall be blessed for ever."

Dick said he'd like for me to be in the Philippines by September. I had *no* idea how that could happen! I did know that our faithful God who had led this far would certainly not let us down now.

Most missionaries do some "deputation" to discover support, but as a single girl I didn't feel I could go to churches and say, "I'm going to work with servicemen, wouldn't you like to support me?" And besides, where would I start? OCSC was an unknown baby mission with three missionaries! One friend, Marie, offered to send $10 a month (she still supports us!) and Dick had about $100 a month in promised support. Among several things we asked God to do was to increase Dick's support, and month by month it inched up.

My Uncle Andrew came to me one day and said, "How would you like to work your way to the Philippines? We can go down to San Pedro and talk to my cousin-in-law who is the captain of a Norwegian freighter and see if he can sign you on as a 'work-away.'" When the ship came into port we went, and the captain said he would let me know after his three month trip to the Far East. God gave me the assurance He'd get me there that way before the captain let me know. I learned, after we were at sea, that had he not had his full quota of 12 passengers, he could not have signed me on as an extra stewardess. Previously, he had not had 12 passengers, but this trip he did.

– MARGARET PATTY, *LOOKING BACK*

OCTOBER 23, 1955

DEAR FOLKS,

NOPE, I'M NOT MARRIED YET. A COUPLE CROOKS DOWN AT THE CITY HALL MANAGED TO GET OUR APPLICATIONS FOR A LICENSE ALL FOULED UP, AND THEN WANTED SOME MONEY UNDER THE TABLE TO GET IT STRAIGHTENED OUT. I REFUSED, AND THEN FOUND OUT A COUPLE DAYS LATER THAT THEY WEREN'T EVEN AUTHORIZED TO WORK ON MARRIAGE LICENSES. WHEN I FOUND THE RIGHT PEOPLE IT WAS TAKEN CARE OF WITHOUT ANY TROUBLE, BUT WE HAVE TO WAIT 11 DAYS TO PICK IT UP SO WE CAN'T GET MARRIED YET.

MARGARET'S SHIP DIDN'T GET HERE UNTIL 11:30 FRIDAY NIGHT, OCT. 14, AND WE HAVE BEEN BUSY MOST OF THE TIME SINCE THEN GETTING HER THROUGH IMMIGRATION AND HER BAGGAGE THROUGH CUSTOMS. FRIDAY, A NAVY CHIEF AND HIS WIFE DROVE DOWN FROM SUBIC IN A CHEVY CARRY-ALL AND TOOK US AND A LOAD OF BAGGAGE BACK TO OLONGAPO. MARGARET STAYED WITH THEM OVER NIGHT, THEN WE SPENT MOST OF YESTERDAY UN-PACKING AND PUTTING THINGS AWAY. MANAGED TO FIGHT OUR WAY ONTO THE LAST BUS BACK TO MANILA LAST NIGHT AT 5:30. BEFORE WE GOT OUT OF OLONGAPO THEY HAD TO STOP AND PUT ON ANOTHER UNIVERSAL JOINT. IT WAS RAINING HARD AND THE ROADS WERE PRETTY SOFT IN SPOTS, BUT THE REST OF THE TRIP WENT PRETTY WELL, AND MARGARET SEEMS TO ENJOY THIS MODE OF TRAVEL.

NETTIE MILLER CAME HOME FROM THE HOSPITAL LAST TUESDAY WITH A NEW BABY GIRL, SO MARGARET HAS BEEN HELPING OUT SOME HERE IN THE MANILA HOME. I PLAN TO GO BACK TO OLONGAPO ON WED. TO SEE SOME FEL-LOWS OFF WHO ARE LEAVING FOR THE STATES, AND MEET A LOT OF OTHERS WHO ARE JUST ARRIVING. WILL THEN COME BACK TO MANILA SUNDAY NIGHT, AND WILL ON MONDAY NIGHT BE JOINED BY THE LORD TO THE FINEST GIRL HE EVER MADE. I CAN'T HELP BUT BE AMAZED AT HOW NATURALLY SHE FITS INTO EVERYTHING HERE. IT IS CERTAINLY EVIDENT THAT THE LORD HAS PRE-PARED HER FOR THE MINISTRY HERE. MUST CLOSE NOW AND THINK THROUGH THE MESSAGE FOR TONIGHT.

LOVE,
DICK

a trip to the market ⸺

Last night, as I bounced along for 3 hours on the unpadded seat of a bus coming back from Manila over a very rough and dusty road, I tried to remember what it used to be like to go shopping in the States. The memory seems to have grown rather dim and I've probably forgotten the unpleasant aspects, but I vaguely recall being able to drop in at a not too distant market and in a few minutes pick up most everything needed in the line of food – without even haggling over the price of each item. Being able to pick out just what you need at the hardware store or lumber yard is another dim, but haunting memory.

– DICK PATTY, APRIL 8, 1959

(L-R) LOU HARRISON, LARRY HOWARD, BUDDY SCHOFIELD, AND BEN CADY

In 1956, the Tarkingtons arrived in Manila to direct the Center and allow Jesse and Nettie to return to Denver and direct the Mission. During the five years of ministry in the Philippines, Tark had the privilege of having men like Buddy Schofield and Lou Harrison active in his Center. Also, he worked with Sid Hendry, who was assisting Dick Patty at Subic, in laying the foundation to open the work by Chuck and Janie Hall at Clark Air Base.

SUBIC SERVICE CENTER
P. O. Box 13, Olongapo
Zambales, Philippines
May *10,* 1956

Hello there,

The *SMILES* on the face of these two servants of Christ are especially for *you.* We are *so* thankful that God has allowed us to work together here, and are grateful to each of you for your prayers that have been answered so exceeding abundantly toward us.

The *SIGN* gives you a little clue as to what goes on inside that building. The LOUNGE is really looking sharp now with the new raw silk drapes Margaret finished recently. "Boy, I never expected to find a place like this in Olongapo!" is the typical exclamation of a fellow coming in for the first time. Up-to-date stateside magazines (both Christian & secular), disc recorder for 'talking letters home,' piano, and soft chairs all invite a sailor to stick around for at least part of the evening instead of making the usual round of bars and clubs. But the lounge is really 'home' for a growing group of Christian fellows, and two nights a week it turns into a class room for an hour or so as we dig into the Word. Extra chairs have to be rounded up to handle the 30 to 50 who gather for the singing, testimonies, and short gospel message of the Sunday afternoon vespers.

The GAMES seem to be especially appreciated by the fleet sailors who have been cramped up on a ship for several weeks. In spite of the oppresive heat, the current ping pong tournament is keeping both tables busy much of the time.

Yet the CHOW continues to be the big attraction. In fact, it looks like Margaret will soon be famous through-out the Pacific fleet for her good cooking. The average group of fellows that show up for the Sunday afternoon dinners has increased in size at the rate of better than 10 a month. Last week it reached 67! Last month, along with the sandwiches, cookies, etc. served over our little canteen counter, the fellows ate 1607 bananas and drank 109 gallons of punch.

The *SOULS* of some of these men have recently passed from death to Life. What a thrill it has been to see their lives literally transformed by God. And the transforming work is continuing in the lives of these and many of the older Christians. We are sure that the growing stability and fruitfulness of their lives are bringing a good deal of joy to the Lord.

The five-day Servicemen's Bible Conference at the Manila home has just drawn to a close. The outstanding missionaries who taught the classes were surely used of God to bless and strengthen the life of each man there. Two young Christian couples here at Subic, with whom we have been enjoying fellowship, offered to stand by at the Center, so Margaret and I were able to attend, along with 15 sailors from here. Margaret helped Nettie Miller in the kitchen, and I had the privilege of teaching a daily class on the Quiet Time and other practical aspects of Christian living.

The theme of the conference was, "Here am I, send me" (Isa. 6:8), and we are confident that, should the Lord tarry, the years ahead will find many of these same men out proclaiming the Gospel of Christ on various mission fields of the world. In the mean time most of them recognize that the barracks or ship where they are right now is a definite mission field. One of the fellows at the conference told how he had been led to Christ on Cubi Point a couple months ago by another Sea Bee who was also at the conference.

But a true picture of the work here would have to include the *SORROW* of our hearts over the spiritual indifference of so many of the men we meet day by day. It seems that all moral restraint is cast aside over here, and boys from good homes, and even some from good churches, are dissipating their lives in riotous living. Please pray for us, that we will be able to present the Gospel to them "not in word only, but in power."

Yours in the bonds of Christ,

Dick & Margaret

I Chron 16:27

ALASKA

THE ANCHORAGE CHRISTIAN SERVICEMEN'S HOME
ANCHORAGE, ALASKA
DIRECTORS: HARLEY AND MIRIAM DOW

As a skiing serviceman in Alaska, Harley Dow saw the spiritual need among service-men. After release from the army, graduation from college, marriage, becoming the father of two fine sons, and a trip up the Alcan Highway in a 1950 Dodge, Harley again finds himself in Alaska, as God's servant among servicemen.

This home has been in operation for more than a year, and men from Elmendorf Air Force Base have found their way to this haven, and some have found peace of heart. Terrific battles have been waged as Satan bids high for these men. Some battles have resulted in victory; some in defeat as men have resisted God.

The activities sponsored by the home are varied. From skiing trips to ping-pong in the parlor, the fellows find their interests. The strongest emphasis is put on the spirtual aspects of life. Long before winter's nine-or-ten-o'clock-sunrise, the Dows have arisen and met their Lord in prayer. Prayer with the men has had many rewards. Bible class-es, personal counseling, the weekly Gospel Hour, and devotions at mealtimes have had an impact on the lives of men. The Lord has provided the necessities for running this home. The Dows' faith in the Lord has been challenging and invigorating to many. Larger quarters are imperative. Pray for this, and for the ministry among the men in Anchorage, the "city whose bar is a mile long."

O.C.S.C. Bulletin, Winter 1959

MY TESTIMONY

by Harley Dow, 1957

It was a cold, clear, but windy evening as we found ourselves in Chicago with a five-hour layover while enroute to Alaska via Seattle. With this time on our hands, my buddy and I decided to take a walk and see a little of the big city.

As we walked, I looked up. A large sign caught my eye: VICTORY CENTER. Out of curiosity and in hopes there would be something to eat, we went in. Much to our surprise, we found more than we expected. We got our snack, plus some good wholesome recreation. But best of all, as we were in the midst of a game of ping-pong, a Mr. Newman approached me and said, "Soldier, are you sure you are ready to go to Heaven?" I had to give him a negative answer because I did not have the witness of the Spirit to give me that assurance. He asked me if I would like to make sure.

We went over to one of the lounges and there this man, by the power of the Holy Spirit, led me to the One who is the Way, the Truth, and the Life, Jesus Christ. He encouraged me to read my Bible and to pray every day.

All too soon our five hours were gone. We headed back to the base. My buddy was the same kind of person, but I was a new creature in Christ Jesus.

HARLEY AND MIRIAM DOW WITH CHILDREN TIM, DAVID, AND PETER

WHAT GOD HATH WROUGHT IN ALASKA

by Miriam Dow, 1958

"Great is the Lord and greatly to be praised!"

From July first, when we arrived in Anchorage, to September fifth, when we occupied the Home, we watched the Lord move men and things to get this Home ready for His work.

When first we arrived, we had no idea how to go about getting a house that would be adequate for our purpose. Step by step we saw the Lord indicate to us His plan. Now we are occupying a house near Elmendorf Air Force Base, which the owner remodeled to our plan! Marvelously, and so graciously, we saw everything provided! We praise the Lord.

The opening and dedication service for this God-provided Home here in Anchorage was held on September 16th. It was as if our heavenly Father Himself spoke to each person as he entered, whispering, "This is my choice," because the facial expressions carried God's confirmation to us.

Harley gave a brief summary from the days of our salvation to this very night . . . Harley and I were asked to stand side by side as a prayer was offered and we were again dedicated to God for His use. We shall never forget those precious few moments. Major Thompson brought a short message. This man is taking a positive stand for the Lord on the base and needs your prayers even as other Christian fellows who seek to live a testimony before this wicked world. At the close of the message, Rev. James Riley gave an appropriate invitation. Since this is a "Home away from Home," the theme of the message was "Home," speaking of course of our Heavenly Home. Pastor Riley invited the sinners to "come Home."

THE MOST IMPORTANT PERSON IN A VITAL
CHRISTIAN LIFE IS JESUS CHRIST. EVERY DECISION IS
TEMPERED AND ADJUSTED WITH THE DESIRE TO
ENLARGE THE VICTORY OF CHRIST IN THE LIFE.
OUR AIM AMONG SERVICEMEN IS TO:
1. BE THAT VITAL CHRISTIAN,
2. BUILD VITAL CHRISTIANS.

– CHUCK HALL, WRITING FROM CRISTOBAL, PANAMA IN 1966

PANAMA
CANAL ZONE

<u>CHRISTIAN SERVICEMEN'S CENTER</u>
COROZAL HOSPITAL AREA
BALBOA, CANAL ZONE
DIRECTORS: TOM AND DOTTY HASH,
GORDON AND JUNE GUSTAFSON

<u>CRISTOBAL SERVICEMEN'S CENTER</u>
BLDG. 1205
CRISTOBAL, CANAL ZONE
DIRECTORS: HARLEY AND MIRIAM DOW,
SID HENDRY,
CHUCK AND JANE HALL

BALBOA, 1958

DOTTY: As we entered the stairwell of the large wooden building, the odor of mildew and cockroach drippings assaulted our nostrils. Then we heard wings flapping. Horrified, we watched bats fly around us, angry that we had disturbed their sleep. Little piles of termite dust lay on the wooden stairs. We walked slowly through the former nurses' quarters, closely examining the sixteen rooms, four bathrooms, two stairwells, and eight carports. There was no kitchen – we would need to build one. But other than cleaning and painting and the removal of some walls, it was perfect! Our hearts beat wildly as we returned to the car. There, we bowed our heads, asking the Lord to make this the Christian Servicemen's Home.

We drafted a letter to Governor Seybold, requesting permission to establish a ministry there. Then Mr. Steers, principal financial officer, a general officer of the Panama Canal Company and Comptroller of the Canal Zone Government, arranged an appointment for Tom to make the formal request directly to the governor. Tom will never forget that day.

TOM: Phil accompanied me into the governor's office. I had never seen such a massive desk! The governor, in his immaculate white suit, looked awesome. My knees knocked; my palms were sweaty. After reading my letter and asking many questions, the governor said, "There are all kinds of religious groups wanting permission to locate in the Zone. Why should I authorize your mission to do so?"

At that moment the Lord reminded me that even though the governor was dressed in civilian clothes, he was still a two-star general and a soldier at heart.

"Sir," I said, "you know that when the soldiers get off duty they usually head for the bars, casinos, and prostitutes there at 'the limits' in Panama City. Our mission wants to provide an alternative – a home away from home – where the welcome mat is out, where they can get a home-cooked meal and have Christian fellowship in a loving atmosphere."

"Just where would this home be located?" the governor asked. I handed him the second letter requesting the use of the former nurses' quarters, now vacant and apparently scheduled to be torn down. The governor carefully read the letter and handed it back to me with the comment, "Take it to the executive secretary. He will make arrangements."

As Mr. Steers and I returned to his office, he said, "Tom, do you know what really happened just now? In those few minutes your mission received the governor's approval of housing your ministry in the Canal Zone. This is unique, as no other mission has that privilege! You will have your Christian Servicemen's Home in the Zone as soon as the papers can be processed. Praise the Lord!"

Tom and Dotty Hash
from Fill These Rooms,
recounting the beginning of the Christian
Servicemen's Home in Balboa Canal Zone

On December 7th, 1941, I was on the battleship Tennessee, just in front of the Arizona. That infamous bombing of Pearl Harbor broke up a prayer meeting some of us sailors were having in preparation for Sunday morning Chapel services on our ship.

GORDON GUSTAFSON

GRACE, JUNE, DANNY, CHARLES, GUS, AND VALERIE GUSTAFSON

In February 1963 this three-story concrete building was transferred without obligation to the Overseas Christian Servicemen's Centers by the American Bible Society for our ministry among servicemen based on the Atlantic side of the Canal Zone.

Since their arrival in the Zone in December, Mr. and Mrs. Harley Dow have been living in an apartment in this building, making contacts with servicemen and seeking the Lord's will concerning the most effective way to reach those stationed at the various military bases. (It is in this area that the Army has its Jungle Warfare Training Center.)

The building is located a very short distance from the downtown area where the men spend most of their off-duty hours. With the Lord's blessing, soon this will be a lighthouse for them in the midst of the darkness of the sin-filled streets of Panama.

O.C.S.C. Bulletin, Spring 1963

The Panama Canal

AS SOLDIERS OF CHRIST, WE ARE COMMITTED TO BATTLE AGAINST THE ENEMY OF MEN'S SOULS, IN THE NAME OF OUR VICTORIOUS RISEN CHRIST! ARE YOU INVOLVED IN THIS BATTLE?

— JESSE MILLER, 1966

THE EXPANSION

1960-1970

OUR GREATEST NEED

by Jesse Miller, 1958

During my travels in the time we have been here in the States, the Lord has brought me in touch with many who have said they were faithfully praying for this work among servicemen. I've been asked often regarding the greatest need in this ministry.

MORE WORKERS. More workers who are called of God, and who are willing to trust Him to supply all their needs. That is our greatest need.

Both the Pattys and the Tarkingtons have need for additional workers to carry the load of responsibilities and opportunities.

Clark Field in the Philippines presents another challenge. For years we have prayed that this place might have a Servicemen's Home. At the present there is a group of Christian boys praying that this might come to pass even while they are based there. Then too, there are other places bordering the Pacific which have requested us to send them someone to work among the servicemen. There is no one to send.

As the work progresses in Panama and Alaska, they too will be needing additional workers. God forbid that His work be curtailed because of a lack of willing workers.

"PRAY YE THEREFORE THE LORD OF THE HARVEST,
THAT HE WILL SEND FORTH LABORERS."
MATTHEW 9:38

CHUCK AND JANE HALL WITH JANET, JEANNI, AND STEVEN

In 1950, I was an airman based at the U.S. Military Port of Manila. Seeking satisfaction, I began dabbling in questionable activities which could have led to most serious repercussions, but for the Lord's intervention. The unrest of my heart continued. Working with me was a big strapping athletic man who everybody called "Tark." It was through the personal witness and life of Tark that I began to see the insignificance of this life and to hunger for the Lord. Jesse Miller was teaching the Bible classes on the base at that time, and it was through this ministry I made the final decision to accept Christ as my Savior.

Through faithful teaching of the Scriptures for about a year after my conversion, I began to grow in the Lord. I found myself unsatisfied with an ordinary Christian life, and not satisfied with any life but that of witnessing and living for Christ. I surrendered my life to the Lord for full time service and have sought to prepare myself for that purpose. Now my formal education is coming to a halt, but my heart longs for more of the fellowship with the One who bought me, for I have tasted that the Lord is good.

CHUCK HALL, 1959

APRIL 1963

Dear Friends,

"The Tom-Toms thumped straight on all night, and the darkness shuddered around me like a living, feeling thing." Night after night these words of Amy Carmichael's ring in our hearts as the drums from the nearby nightclubs beat into our ears endlessly. They are a constant reminder to us that Satan is bidding high for the hearts of the American boys we love, and that we're in a tremendous spiritual warfare with him.

Dick and I almost weep for joy to hear some of you are remembering us faithfully before the Throne of Grace. Because you pray, God uses our lives for His glory, and we do thank you so much.

These have been full months. The work on the building continues as rapidly as health, strength, and funds permit, but there are many months of work yet ahead. After "camping" in our kitchen for over a year, we finally have kitchen cabinets, and today the linoleum is being laid, so from a woman's point of view, great progress has been made! The downstairs, which will eventually be game room, canteen, lounge, and office, is being worked on now. Perhaps the game room will be useable within the next month. The three Binghams are in one bedroom, and we four are in another, but we hope to spread out before too long.

The fellows *are* enjoying their new "home away from home," and we thoroughly enjoy having them as a part of the family. The Lord has given several choice opportunities recently to talk with men who don't know Him. We know of no higher privilege than to explain to them how dearly the great God of the universe loves *them* and gave the life of His very own Son that He might have *their* fellowship and friendship.

Sundays have brought over 70 for Vesper Service and dinner several times lately. This includes several families that are close to us because of Dick's couples' class, the women's class, or the base choir that I've been directing.

The need for sharing our home with these men becomes daily more evident. When we saw many of you in 1960, there were just over 100 nightclubs and bars in this two-mile stretch of town. Now there are 200, with several more under construction. The atmosphere is intense with evil; "the most wicked port in the Far East," according to most of the men.

But God is answering your prayers. The nightclubs to the south of us mentioned in our last newsletter haven't been opened, but neither have they been torn down, so continue to pray about this threat. The gambling hall on

> "The Subic Center is supported by voluntary gifts from interested friends and churches. The major portion usually comes from servicemen and former servicemen who have spent time here. This building has been constructed and furnished without the incurring of any indebtedness at the cost of $105,000. Over 80% of this has been given by servicemen."

DICK PATTY

our east continues to operate quietly. Just after lunch yesterday we watched the place being surrounded by Philippine Constabulary men armed with automatic weapons. They evidently didn't find whom they wanted, and left late in the afternoon without firing a shot. Probably unrelated is the rumor that a man was murdered there several weeks ago. Murders are frequent in Olongapo, but are never publicized.

Do pray for continued health for us, and for spiritual victory in the lives of the men and women to whom we minister.

Yours and His,
Margaret and Dick

SUBIC CENTER
DEDICATION SERVICE

by Dick Patty, May 1964

"Hitherto hath the Lord helped us."

During the summer of 1954, Jesse Miller, director of the Manila Christian Servicemen's Home, Dick Patty, C.P. Tarkington, and Tom Hash met in Chicago for the formation of Overseas Christian Servicemen's Centers, a non-profit, interdenominational, missionary corporation. This organization now sponsors three centers in the Philippines, one in Okinawa, and two in Panama, with a home office in Denver, Colorado.

In February, 1955, Dick joined sixteen fellows in the little hut up on Cubi Point to labor with them in bringing to reality the vision they had held for many months. They had no money, no equipment, no building, but great confidence in God's purpose and faithfulness to bless and use them.

Space was finally leased in a building across from the Public Market; furniture was constructed in the hobby shop; and the doors of the Subic Service Center were opened July 1, 1955. From time to time other provisions were made that contributed to the effectiveness of the operation. Gifts from friends in the States made possible the purchase of a stove, refrigerator, piano, and some smaller items which a C.B. battalion delivered. Even more important to the future work was the favorable response of Margaret Olsen, a nurse in Los Angeles, to the tape recorded proposal she received from the Center director.

Margaret was able to get employment as a stewardess on a Norwegian freighter and worked her way across the Pacific to Manila to become Mrs. Dick Patty in October, 1955.

Within a couple of years, the need for larger facilities became a matter of serious prayer and continued to be for months that grew into years. The present lot was acquired in January of 1959. Construction got underway early in 1961, and one apartment was completed sufficiently for occupation by the end of that year. The Center was limited to this apartment for nearly a year, then gradually expanded to include most of the second floor of the building as construction progressed. Today, the downstairs recreation area, canteen, lounge, and office are being opened for the use of the servicemen.

In March of 1959, Sid Hendry joined the Pattys on the Center staff. He was assisted by missionaries Ray and Alice Kalbach during the Pattys' visit to the States in 1960. Sid was replaced by current staff members Bob and Dorothy Bingham in late October of 1962 and is now at the Center in Cristobal, Panama.

The Subic Center is supported by voluntary gifts from interested friends and churches. The major portion usually comes from servicemen and former servicemen who have spent time here. This building has been constructed and furnished without the incurring of any indebtedness at the cost of $105,000. Over 80% of this has been given by servicemen. There has never been an offering taken at the Center nor have funds been solicited by letter or person. The provision of these facilities has been a satisfying confirmation that the confidence placed over nine years ago in the purpose and faithfulness of God was not misplaced!

ARRIVING IN THE PHILIPPINES

BY BOB BINGHAM

In late summer 1958, Erv Meyer called me one day and said that he had heard a man speaking at a conference at the Navigators. He said that he wanted to start meeting with him. The man was Jesse Miller. I said that I wanted to go too. I started meeting with Erv and Jesse on Wednesday evenings. We were studying the Tabernacle with Jesse Miller. Erv and I would do original research from the Scriptures and Erv would work through the Scofield notes. I really learned a lot and we also contributed to Jesse Miller's study on the Tabernacle.

OCSC is a faith mission and we had to raise our financial support. When people knew that Dorothy and I were going to be missionaries with OCSC, several churches and individuals came up to me and said, "You can count on us for support." It was really humbling.

My mother gave us the money to pay for our transportation from Denver to the Philippines. It was very hard for her since we were taking away her only grandchild, Deanna, who at that time was just 13 months old.

We left Denver in our car and a U-Haul trailer with all of our belongings that we were going to ship. We drove to Oakland, California and then to San Francisco where we stayed at the Home of Peace, a place that was designed to assist missionaries going overseas. They put us up and then packed our things for shipment. We stayed there 5 or 6 days, until our ship was ready for us to board. We sailed on the President Lines, the S.S. President Jefferson. It was a freighter and at that time freighters were allowed to take 8 passengers.

When we got to the Philippines, we stopped in Subic Bay first. Sid Hendry met us; we were to relieve him so he could go back to the States on furlough. After good fellowship we got back on the ship that night and went to Manila to disembark there with our cargo.

Ben Cady was supposed to meet us and then take us and all our stuff to the Servicemen's Center at Cavite City for overnight and then the next day we would get our baggage through customs. But he was sick and in the hospital with an infection, so Connie Cady came and picked us up. It was nightfall by now and she wanted me to drive from Manila to Cavite which is a thin peninsula sticking out in Manila Bay. It was one of the wildest drives I have ever driven because it was just a two-lane road with people sitting along the side of the road. There were jeepneys driving without headlights. It was really quite something! We got to Cavite safely and Connie put us up overnight. The next day we went and got our baggage out of customs. Sid Hendry was there and helped us get from there up north to Olongapo where we were going to spend the next couple years.

I remember getting up one morning at Subic and our house-help, Connie, came over with tears in her eyes and said, "Your president has been killed." That was the day President Kennedy was assassinated. It was hard to believe from way over in the Philippines. Our helpers were really shook up over it and of course we were too.

There were a lot of sailors and marines during this time that would come and go. The fleet would come into Subic Bay for a week or so, and there'd be hundreds, sometimes thousands of sailors on the street at night. Olongapo had about 350 bars, clubs and houses of prostitution. It was not unusual for half the ship's crew to come back after a night on the town with a venereal disease.

Olongapo was considered the worst town in the world that the Navy put in to port. On Sundays or during the week, we'd drive through the town and many of the prostitutes would be dressed up in their finery. Our preschooler, Deanna, would wonder if they were getting ready to go to church or coming back from church.

I had the opportunity to teach a Bible class at the Center which went pretty well. But I was not real happy with it because I didn't get a whole lot of discussion. That all changed after listening to Howard Hendricks, who came to the Philippines for a summer to teach at FEBIAS Bible College in Manila. Just before he left to go back to the States, Dick Patty made arrangements for him to speak to all the OCSC missionaries and then be the key note speaker for one of our Baguio Bible conferences.

Howard Hendricks met with us at Clark Air Base at the Christian Servicemen's Home. He made a very interesting statement that transformed my whole teaching experience. He said that the problem with most teachers is that they want the pupils to know how much the teacher knows, rather than being concerned about the pupil's learning. He said, in order for the pupils to understand, they need to put concepts into their own words. If the teacher wants discussion, he or she needs to be patient enough to allow the students time to discuss and ask questions. That really struck me and that transformed my whole teaching method. From that time on, teaching was a wonderful experience for me. I will always be grateful to Howard Hendricks and Dick Patty for that time.

Lorene Glynn served at the O.C.S.C. Home Office in Denver from October 1962 to December 1964, and then at the Subic Service Center in the Philippines with the Pattys, Cadys, Hendricks, and Harrisons from January 1965 to May 1968. She then assisted missionaries in Thailand and Japan before moving to work at the Home Office in 1969. Lorene continues to minister to the military to this day.

O.C.S.C. Bulletin

Spring — 1964

SENDING LABORERS

BEHIND THE SCENES IN EVERY MISSION OFFICE ARE THOSE WHO HANDLE THE MUNDANE AFFAIRS TO FACILITATE MISSIONARY ENDEAVOR. GOD HAS BLESSED THE O.C.S.C. OFFICE WITH EXCELLENT WORKERS DURING THE YEARS.

LAST DECEMBER, ERVIN MEYER, WHO HAD WORKED AS O.C.S.C. BOOKKEEPER, ARRIVED IN OKINAWA TO HELP THE TARKINGTONS. ERV HAD BECOME WELL ACQUAINTED WITH THE ORGANIZATION AND PURPOSES OF O.C.S.C.

THIS SPRING THE LORD INDICATED THAT ANOTHER WORKER, LORENE GLYNN, IS MARKED FOR SERVICE OVERSEAS. O.C.S.C. MISSIONARIES IN THE PHILIPPINES HAVE ASKED HER TO COME BY THE END OF JULY TO HELP IN SECRETARIAL AND BOOKKEEPING DUTIES. MISS GLYNN HAS ACCEPTED THIS AS GOD'S DIRECTION FOR THE NEXT STEP IN HER LIFE.

AFTER GRADUATION FROM BUSINESS COLLEGE MISS GLYNN WAS ON HER WAY UP IN THE SECRETARIAL WORLD. THEN, SHE HEARD GOD'S CALL, ACCEPTED HIM AS SAVIOUR AND LORD, AND OBEYED HIS CALL TO PREPARE FOR MISSIONARY SERVICE. WHILE IN BIBLE SCHOOL, SHE OFFERED HER SECRETARIAL ABILITIES IN THE O.C.S.C. OFFICE. MANY TEDIOUS TASKS SHE HAS PERFORMED CHEERFULLY AS UNTO THE LORD--EACH A PREPARATION FOR A FUTURE WORK.

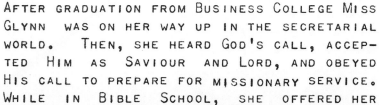

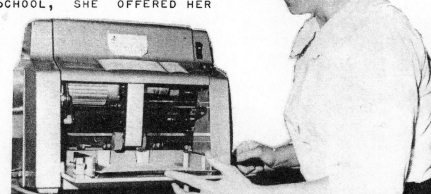

Jan Lahman, Barb France, and Dennis and Betty Ortman served as O.C.S.C. missionaries at Faith Academy in Manila.

TOP: JANET LAHMAN ON A SHIP TO THE PHILIPPINES IN 1966, WHERE SHE TAUGHT AT FAITH ACADEMY FOR OVER 30 YEARS.

LEFT: BARB FRANCE'S ENGAGEMENT TO WYCLIFFE MISSIONARY, JIM MUSGROVE. THEY WERE MARRIED IN JUNE 1967 AND CONTINUED TO TEACH AT FAITH ACADEMY WITH WYCLIFFE.

RIGHT: DENNIS AND BETTY ORTMAN

DENNIS WAS DISCIPLED UNDER DICK AND MARGARET'S MINISTRY AT SUBIC. HE AND BETTY RETURNED TO THE PHILIPPINES WITH O.C.S.C. IN 1967.

SANGLEY POINT

Begun in Manila in 1952, moved to Cavite City in 1958, and closed in 1967 when the base closed.

APRIL 22, 1961

"This is the day the Lord hath made, we will rejoice and be glad in it."
Yes, tonight we arrive in the land where I started LIVING! We just
passed Corregidor about 1930 . . . many fishing boats. Finally docked
at 2230 and were welcomed by a group of missionaries including
Tarks, Sid, Halls, Brooks and others. Back home at last!!! We went
to Cavite for the night. Connie thought that the geckos which scooted
up the wall were mice so was greatly relieved that they were harmless.
Praise the Lord for His establishing the Home here in Cavite. Could
hardly sleep for the excitement.

- EXCERPT FROM BEN CADY'S LOGBOOK

HAVING BABIES IN THE PHILIPPINES

by Connie Cady

After nearly a month on a freighter, the Pattys and the Cadys were finally at their destination. Both Margaret and I were pregnant. Alma Tarkington had found a doctor in Cavite City for me.

Several months later, when I arrived at her little clinic/hospital for Randy's birth, there was a flurry of activity and excitement as I was the first American to give birth there. Then it came time to go to their little delivery room. I was so surprised that even the houseboys and other help were in the delivery room, just in case something went wrong.

One and a half years later when our son, Doug, was born, it was only the doctor and me in the delivery room, and this time I was the nervous one!

Image on left: Connie and Ben Cady with children Randy and Janelle
Image on right: the Cady family with the addition of sons Doug and Craig

DEAD IN THE WATER

by Dotty Hash in Fill These Rooms

The S.S. President Jefferson slipped away from the dock in the early morning hours of December 1, 1963. Even with a wool blanket and Tom's arms wrapped tightly around me, the biting, cold wind chilled us to the bone as we stood on the deck watching the Golden Gate Bridge disappear into the distance. We wondered what adventures lay ahead.

Within a few hours, our captain informed us that one boiler was not functioning properly so our speed had been reduced. We plodded slowly onward for 760 miles. Just after retiring one evening, the captain bolted into our rooms. "Secure those children! We're adrift at sea!" The engines had been turned off and dismantled while we waited for parts to be sent from Los Angeles. I soon learned that a ship "dead in the water" is at the mercy of the ocean – lying in the trough of the swell, rocking constantly as the waves rise and fall. For the rest of the night, with each roll, a chair or suitcase slid across the room. We could hear dishes breaking in the galley. Eventually the movable items were secured, and all became strangely quiet.

The next morning we gingerly made our way to the galley. I, along with four-year-old David, had been assigned to sit at the captain's table for the voyage, while Tom, Lori and Danny were at the other end of the dining room. I put David into the high chair beside me, but with the first roll of the ship, his chair slid across the room. Panicking, a steward jumped to catch him, and then promptly tied

his chair to mine with a dishtowel. We bounced around with the waves for two days.

The ship hobbled along for twenty [more] hours; then flashes appeared on the horizon. The captain hurried from the bridge to the radio shack. Beep, beep, beep – over the radio came the wonderful news that we were approaching the Coast Guard ship and they had our long-awaited bearing on board! This being an emergency, a Coast Guard plane had delivered the part.

The ship pulled up to the dock in Manila Bay at 7 a.m. on Christmas morning 1963. What joy to see Chuck and Jane Hall, Ben Cady and a few of the fellows there to meet us. By 10:30 we had cleared customs with our cabin baggage and were on our way to Clark Air Force Base, three hours away. Christmas dinner was waiting at the Christian Servicemen's Home when we arrived and was followed by receptions for us in the evening. With couples and single men, the group numbered around sixty, many of whom were new believers.

The ministry at Clark was actually begun by an Air Force sergeant and his wife who had been challenged during the Bible conference at the Manila home in 1956. As a result, Cecil Allen, his wife, and six children opened their home at Clark to the servicemen for fellowship and Bible study. The normal tour of duty for servicemen overseas was two years, but the Allens extended for an additional two years in order to serve the Lord in this way.

After Sid Hendry arrived to assist Dick Patty at Subic in March 1959, he rode a motor scooter the fifty miles to Clark on Mondays to teach a Bible class and to challenge the growing group. He wrote to the home office, "The group of Christians is growing in number and in the Lord . . . There are some seventeen in attendance. Each one is praying specifically for someone to come . . . Such hungry hearts I have never seen! They are like sheep without a shepherd."

It was during this time that Ralph Porter, an airman stationed at Clark, came to know Christ as his Savior. Ralph and Wilma later became

missionaries with OCSC and serve faithfully to this day.

Chuck and Jane Hall were God's answer to the prayers of that little group. They arrived in the Philippines on August 2, 1960, shortly after the Allens rotated back to the States. The group had rented a house for them, paying the rent for two months in advance, had hired two house girls, and even bought a few pieces of furniture.

The Halls were virtually on their honeymoon when they arrived. Their first meal in this, their first home, was eaten on packing crates covered with a cloth, a romantic

candle glowing in the center. Later Jane admitted the reason for the elegant atmosphere was to disguise the steak she had burned. But Chuck was duly impressed.

In a short time, they knew the house was too small to carry on a growing ministry. They found a location in Embassy Court, a secure compound along the perimeter fence, just outside the main gate of the base. There were about fourteen homes in the compound, surrounded by a barbed wire fence. There was an entrance gate into the compound, where guards on twenty-four hour duty checked everyone coming through. Dispersed among the homes were three guard shacks where armed men watched throughout the night hours. The Halls negotiated with the owner of the compound to have a home built, customized to fit the needs of the ministry.

The two-story, 1900 square foot building had four bedrooms, a sala (sitting room) and bath upstairs, with a kitchen, dining room, living room, and small office downstairs. Within a year of occupancy, the Halls realized it was simply too small, so at their own expense (the building was rented) and with the help of the airmen, they added a large screened-in porch on three sides. When we arrived, the construction was complete, but it still needed interior finishing.

For the next week Tom and I followed Chuck and Jane around like puppy dogs, eager to learn as much as we could. The most confusing to me was shopping – bartering for everything, knowing where to get this and that and what to look out for. Angeles City, the town near us, had 90,000 people but no paved streets. It was full of open shops, calesas (colorful horse-drawn carts for hire), jeepneys (World War II jeeps converted into colorful taxis or buses), and pedicabs (tricycles with seating for two people on the back).

The climate and culture were similar to what we knew in Panama because both countries had been under Spanish rule for many years in the past. The cost of living was inexpensive compared to the States. I could have my hair done for thirty-five cents. Anything imported was very high, so we lived solely on local goods. Tropical fresh fruits and vegetables were available in abundance and cheap. Jane, a wonderful teacher, was very patient with me.

The three weeks we overlapped with the Halls were hectic, and the day we drove them to Manila to board their plane for the U.S., I was fearful. The ministry was thriving and healthy. Chuck and Jane were dearly loved. Could we really carry on in their place?

After the Halls cleared emigration, the group of friends who had come to bid them farewell sat in the lunchroom at the airport, talking. Wanting desperately to squeeze out every bit of helpful information from Jane that I could, I solemnly asked, "Jane, if it were possible, what is the one thing you would change during this term in the Philippines?"

Not missing a beat, she quipped, "I'd raise up perfume supporters – someone to send me a new bottle of perfume every month!" That was Jane. I loved and admired her greatly and was deeply saddened when the Lord took her home years later after a long bout with cancer.

(L-R): Dotty, Lori, David, Tom, and Danny Hash

GOD'S MIRACULOUS PROVISION

BY CONNIE CADY

In the early years of OCSC/Cadence, the three Centers/Houses in the Philippines worked together twice a year for a Bible Conference at Camp John Hay in the cooler mountain climate of Baguio, Philippines. The night before we were to go to one of these conferences, because of unexpected car bills and other unexpected expenditures, we had absolutely no money.

The solution for me was to just stay home with our two small children, but Ben insisted that I was going. I replied, "When Margaret and the other wives put their money together for marketing, I wouldn't have anything, and of course they will take pity on me and pay for me." His answer was, "Those who trust in the Lord won't be ashamed" (Psalm 25:3).

The next morning we piled in our van along with three young sailors. At Manila, we checked our mailbox for checks or money. Nothing! Then we drove to pick up one of the missionary speakers who was riding with us. Secretly, I thought that he might be the one to pay for the gas. But when he met us, he said he was performing a Chinese wedding and would come up later. So Ben drove to the nearest filling station and asked to be filled up. For some reason, he disappeared (maybe praying in the bathroom). One of the sailors paid for the gas. We were at least going to make it to Baguio!

Shortly after we arrived, Sid Hendry gave Ben money to help with our conference expenses and throughout the week others gave us much more money. Yes, "Those who trust in the Lord won't be ashamed."

Last night, a man came to the Home who had been out to see us off and on for the last six months, but never showed an interest in spiritual things. When he arrived he immediately told me he wanted to talk to me. He stated this: "God sent me here tonight to talk with you. I have professed to believe for seven years, but tonight I know that I have never known God and I do need help." I simply showed him a few promises from the Word and he, in simple faith, trusted the Lord. Do continue to pray because such victories are in answer to prayer only.

C.P. Tarkington, 1959

OKINAWA

KADENA CHRISTIAN CENTER (THE HARBOR)
NEAR GATE 3, KADENA AIR BASE
KOZA, OKINAWA
DIRECTORS: C.P. AND ALMA TARKINGTON,
RAY AND ALICE KALBACH,
RALPH AND WILMA PORTER

HANSEN CHRISTIAN CENTER
4393 AZA-KIN
KIN-CHO, OKINAWA
DIRECTORS: RAY AND ALICE KALBACH,
RALPH AND WILMA PORTER

KADENA

A Christian military family based on Okinawa has sacrificially given their private home near Kadena Air Base for the work of O.C.S.C. among servicemen.

When our missionaries, the Tarkingtons, arrived in Okinawa last November, they rented temporary living quarters and began contacting servicemen, chaplains, and civilians. Realizing an open door of ministry near any of some fifteen military bases, they sought the Lord for clear guidance as to His location for the Christian Servicemen's Center.

The Lord's answer came in the gift of the house on the main road to the air base. The Tarkingtons then made arrangements to purchase the house next door.

The addition of a two-story unit between the two houses will provide the necessary facilities for a wide ministry among the more than 50,000 Americans based on this Island Fortress.

(L-R) JO CAROL, TARK, TIMOTHY, LENA BETH, AND ALMA TARKINGTON

Tark and Alma pioneered the O.C.S.C. Ministry on Okinawa. During their first term they saw God build the Christian Center debt free and dedicated in 1964.

During their second term while continuing to direct the Kadena ministry, with the help of Ralph and Wilma Porter, Tark bought an old nightclub, the "Ammy," with funds raised on Okinawa, to double the size and see the Hansen Christian Center opened under the leadership of Ray Kalbach.

OUR FATHER'S MISSION FOR RALPH & WILMA PORTER

By Ralph and Wilma Porter

[Editor's Note: We have woven Ralph's and Wilma's words together in this recounting of their journey with OCSC/Cadence. We appreciate their distinct voices — Wilma in her solid directness and Ralph in his expressive zeal — both passionate about Christ and his Kingdom.]

W: I met Ralph while a senior at Moody Bible Institute in Chicago. He had just been released from active duty with the army, and recently returned from the Philippines.

R: While stationed at Clark Air Force Base, I was witnessed the Gospel call by Vic Smith, a redeemed soldier, who invited me to a home Bible study led by Sid Hendry, OCSC missionary. Through Sid sharing the Gospel, our Lord's redemption for us through Jesus' Blood sacrifice, I came to know Jesus as Savior and Lord. I went on trips with the young disciples to visit missionaries in the mountains with C.P. Tarkington, OCSC missionary in Manila, and Sid Hendry. I was discipled by Chuck and Jane Hall at the Clark Servicemen's Center where I was with the Army Security Agency.

W: We dated and were married in 1962. Ralph finished Moody in January 1965, just before Rebecca was born. The end of March, we went to Denver to help in the Home Office with Jesse and Nettie Miller. We met other "old timers": the Goodes, Cadys, Woodwards, and Pattys. In August 1965, we were accepted by the mission to start deputation. In February 1968, we went to

Okinawa by way of Sasebo, Japan where we visited the Woodwards and attended Erv Meyer's wedding to Elsie.

We arrived in Okinawa a week before Daniel turned a year old. Here we worked with Ray and Alice Kalbach until they left for Taiwan. That fall, Tark and Alma arrived and we worked together until December 1969. We were asked to go to Subic Bay, PI, to help Tom and Dotty Hash as the Vietnam war brought many aircraft carriers there with their accompanying ships. Rachel was born in the PI where we stayed until May 1971. We spent our first furlough in the States where Ruth was born. We returned to Okinawa in the summer of 1972 where Tark and Alma were leaving for furlough. Ray and Alice Kalbach were at the Hansen Center which he and Tark had established by converting a bar. Abe and Ellen Teeny came to the Hansen Center. I say all of this to emphasize that we were trained by all of the "old timers" and deeply appreciated learning from their examples of faithfulness and endurance.

R: We learned from their sacrificial, loving examples in our Lord Jesus, their faithfulness and endurance

through all the hardships living in the overseas foreign nation and the military communities. We witnessed daily their unwavering love of our Lord Jesus and His Word and their home ministry love of all the young single adults, servicemen husbands, wives, and their children.

W: In 1973, we went to the Hansen Center for two years, then a year of furlough, and then returned to Hansen Center for four years. While there, we were asked by the marines, "Why isn't there something like this in 29 Palms?" We asked, "Where is that?" "In the Mohave Desert of California," commonly known as "29 Stumps in the Heat!" Well, needless to say, after our next Home Assignment, we ended up at 29 Palms for the last 32 years, "loving those marines." Ralph greatly enjoys witnessing to marines and sailors. Meeting strangers and telling them about Jesus is his greatest love.

R: We keep on, like Paul, pressing "toward the mark for the prize of the high calling of God in Christ Jesus" (Philippians 3:14). May we be able to say, "I have fought a good fight, I have finished my course, I have kept the faith. Henceforth there is laid up for me a crown of righteousness, which the Lord, the righteous Judge, shall give me at that day: and not to me only, but unto all them also that love His appearing" (2 Timothy 4:7-8).

We thank you for your prayers as we serve in our Lord Jesus' love of His warriors in the U.S. Armed Forces and the Holy Spirit's working mightily in His redeemed ones for the honor, glory, and praise of our Heavenly Father.

Keep abiding in the intimate, affirming love of our Lord Jesus and His Blood Covenant promises.

Below: C.P. and Alma Tarkington with Ray and Alice Kalbach

Right: Ray and Alice Kalbach with their youngest three chil-

dren: Doug, Wilf, and Lois

HANSEN CHRISTIAN CENTER

THE TESTIMONY
OF A CHAPLAIN

I speak from personal experience, having visited in three of the O.C.S.C. centers and having fellowshipped with fourteen of the O.C.S.C. missionary workers. I cherish wonderful memories of joining with men from my ships to enjoy waffle parties, wiener roasts, treasure hunts, touch football, volleyball, basketball, "naval Olympics," swimming parties, and indoor game nights. Perhaps sailors appreciate such activities more than other servicemen because their "homes of steel" are always noisy and usually rolling and pitching at sea.

Such Christian fellowship is richly enjoyed by the Christian serviceman because he is far from home and he may not have much fellowship on his ship or station. And when such a program is used as a means of making friends of the non-Christian serviceman and "winning a hearing" for the gospel of Christ, then the Christian Servicemen's Center is at its very best! Ungodly servicemen seldom visit church services and evangelistic meetings. But only eternity will reveal how many such have been reached for Jesus Christ through the Christian Servicemen's Centers.

BY CHAPLAIN (LCDR) D. L. MESCHKE, 1964

Chaplain Dave Meschke served on the Board of Directors of O.C.S.C. for many years. Then he served as the General Director of O.C.S.C./Cadence International from 1978 to 1995.

JAPAN

CHRISTIAN SERVICEMEN'S CENTER
YOKOTA, JAPAN
DIRECTORS: RON AND MARLENE BLOUGH

CHRISTIAN SERVICEMEN'S CENTER
1-15 TANIGO-CHO
SASEBO, JAPAN
DIRECTORS: ERV MEYER
LARRY AND LOIS WOODWARD
HAROLD AND EDNA MATOLKA
JOHN AND JOAN HOBSON

CHRISTIAN SERVICEMEN'S CENTER (THE LIGHTHOUSE)
YOKOSUKA, JAPAN
DIRECTORS: ERV AND ELSIE MEYER

YOKOTA, 1961

Ron and Marlene Blough opened a center in Yokota
in 1961 and served there until 1963

YOKOSUKA, 1969

In 1961, when I graduated from college, the Lord led me to work with O.C.S.C./Cadence. At that time the Home Office was in the basement where Jesse and Nettie lived in Lakewood. I worked there two years before going overseas with O.C.S.C. While working with the Millers, I saw them demonstrate integrity and generosity over and over in their kindness to many people. In these, and many other ways, they were always careful to do what God wanted them to do, when He wanted them to do it.

Erv Meyer

SASEBO EXPANDS THE HARD WAY

O.C.S.C. Bulletin, December 1969

On the phone, Larry Woodward said, "Lois, the girls, and some of the fellows had gone to choir practice. Russ and I were in the office. I heard some crackling sounds, and ran out our front door. Sure enough, the other unit of the duplex was on fire!" After calling the fire department, they carried a few futile buckets of water, then directed their energies to moving things out of the Center.

By the time the fire was extinguished, their neighbor's unit had been gutted, the roof was burned off most of their place, and many of their things were water-soaked or damaged by a too-hasty removal from the building.

For months, we have been praying with an increasing burden for larger facilities for this ministry. Houses are small in Japan, and rentals are scarce in Sasebo. Repeated efforts to find a larger building or separate apartment that was large enough for their family met with failure. We prayed even more earnestly. Then, on October 23, the fire – and they had no building at all. Chaplain Parker took them into his home on the base for a few days; then they moved to a cottage at a nearby Christian orphanage. Larry carried on some of his Bible classes by moving them to the base. Further ministry to the fleet continues with projects like the retreat arranged for about 88 men from the USS Coral Sea.

But God is answering the request for more adequate facilities! The land-owner went right to work rebuilding the duplex and has agreed to rent both units to the Woodwards. They hope to be moved in by Christmas.

LARRY AND LOIS WOODWARD

HAROLD AND EDNA MATOLKA

JOHN AND JOAN HOBSON

Erv Meyer opened the Sasebo Center in 1964 and was followed by the Woodwards, the Matolkas, and then the Hobsons.

TAIWAN

HOSPITALITY HOUSE
100 FU LIN ROAD SHIN LIN
TAIPEI, TAIWAN
DIRECTORS: SID AND ANNETTE HENDRY,
RAY AND ALICE KALBACH

WELCOME INN
368 WU CHWAN ROAD
TAICHUNG, TAIWAN
DIRECTORS: CLYDE AND JANE TAYLOR,
GAYNOR AND BARBARA MOLINE

Clyde and Jane Taylor (pictured on the left) opened the Welcome Inn in Taichung, Taiwan. Gaynor and Barbara Moline (pictured on the right) followed in 1968.

TAIPEI HOSPITALITY HOUSE, 1965-1969

The familiar mandarin red gates of the Hospitality House in Taipei, Taiwan, have stood open to American armed forces and U.S. civilian personnel for more than a decade. An informal Christian center, the Hospitality House is located near the American community and offers a convenient and wholesome atmosphere for those who want to relax in a "back-home-like" surrounding.

In March of this year, Sid Hendry arrived at Hospitality House and assumed the duties of Director. The entire work is now the responsibility of O.C.S.C.

On the 7th of August, in Taipei, Taiwan, Sid Hendry and Annette Mitchell were united in marriage. Annette is Margaret Patty's sister. Cyril Brooks from the Philippines performed the ceremony.

O.C.S.C. BULLETIN FALL 1965

SID WITH BABY CAROL

SID AND ANNETTE HENDRY
LARRY AND MARK MITCHELL

LOU AND LINDA HARRISON WITH GREG, BILL KRAMER, LARRY WOODWARD, AND ERV MEYER VISITING
THE HENDRYS IN TAIWAN

VIETNAM

VICTORY VILLA
22-C HUNG VUONG STREET
NHA TRANG, VIETNAM
DIRECTORS: LEMUEL AND MARGE MORGAN

VICTORY VILLA: CENTER OPENS IN NHA TRANG

by Lem and Marge Morgan, 1966

It is our joy to introduce you to Victory Villa! How we wish it were possible for you to drop in for a visit. It's easy to find – only one block from the beach and three blocks from the main entrance to the Air Base – at 22-C Hung Vuong Street.

Since you will probably not be visiting the Center, let us tell you about it. It is the place of the Lord's choice – spacious, bright and cheerful. The extra large front room serves concurrently as lounge, Bible study room, meeting and dining room. In addition, there is an office and bookstore, a guest room, our own bedroom and two bathrooms. As usual in Vietnam, the kitchen is located in another building in the rear.

Although you may not be able to visit the Center, we praise the Lord that many servicemen do. In fact, we recently realized we cannot accommodate many more because our facilities are already crowded. Some come for Bible study, some for fellowship, some for a home-cooked meal, or some other part of our program. Some have even found a "home away from home."

Lem, Marge, Cindy, and Paul Morgan in Vietnam, 1966 and 1968

MARCH 14, 1966

DEAR FRIENDS,

WHEN ASKED TO RETURN THANKS FOR OUR FOOD AT THE DINNER TABLE FOUR-AND-A-
HALF-YEAR-OLD DAVID OFTEN ADDS, "THANK YOU, JESUS, THAT YOU WILL GIVE DADDY A
SAFE TRIP TO VIETNAM, AND THAT HE WON'T GET INTO ANY TROUBLE." THIS SOUNDS LIKE
A PRAYER OF FAITH, AND I LIKE THAT SOUND — IT'S THE KIND OF PRAYER GOD PROMISES
TO ANSWER (MATTHEW 21:22).

ONE OF THE MOST EXCITING EXPERIENCES OF OUR TIME IN THE STATES HAS BEEN TO FIND
OUT HOW MANY OF YOU HAVE BEEN FOLLOWING OUR MINISTRY CAREFULLY AND PRAYING
FOR US FAITHFULLY. AGAIN WE SAY, "THANK YOU!"

YOURS AND HIS,
DICK AND MARGARET PATTY

Dick Patty visiting Lem Morgan in Vietnam in 1966

LEM AND MARGE MORGAN AND SID HENDRY, 1966

People!

The ministry of Cadence is people. People, people, and more people. All kinds of people. And our purpose is to teach and guide them to be faithful followers of Jesus Christ. The only way you can effectively do that is to love them. You may be a great Bible teacher, cook, or communicator, but if you don't love them, it probably won't happen. Love people! Love each other! Love "your" people! Believe me, if you genuinely love them they will come! You may be thoroughly prepared, your facility spiffied up, your food ready, but if you don't love them they will know it – you just can't fake true love. Ask the Lord to give you love!

– DOTTY HASH

TO VIETNAM

BY LOU HARRISON

Linda and I came to OCSC in 1966 right after graduation from Prairie Bible Institute. The Tarkingtons and Cadys had spiritually nurtured me in the Philippines. Linda had been nurtured by missionary parents and a school with a heart for missions.

Since we were both from Southern California, we expected to be assigned to Spain or Italy. Jesse Miller called sometime in 1967 to ask if we wanted to go to "where the action is." We said yes. And he didn't really assign us, but suggested we go to Vietnam. We took it as an assignment from the Lord. Lem and Marge Morgan had been in Vietnam for a couple of years and were then in Nha Trang.

I don't really know how we got to Vietnam. We were completely ignorant – the only Vietnam-experienced workers were already over there – and we had no email and poor phone service overseas in those days. So we had no real chance to get much guidance from the Morgans. Somehow God led us through the process one blind step at a time.

One thing I do vividly recall, is that it was a truck driver in our local church who helped us – rather, actually did the job with my help – pack barrels, crate appliances, and prepare whatever else we needed to open a ministry on the Mekong Delta in Can Tho. We never saw those things again until a year-and-a-half later when they caught up with us on the shipping docks in Bangkok, Thailand. From there we trucked them down to Sattahib. There, everything came out of its container and went to work without a problem, except for cleaning the oil out of the tank of Linda's Maytag washer, which dock workers had rolled end-over-end.

In Vietnam, we caught a plane to Nha Trang to spend some time with the Morgans and get our feet down in the country. The night we arrived at the Morgans' Servicemen's Center the "Tet" New Year celebration was at its peak, with plenty of noisy help from all the weapons available in the country at the time. We were housed in a room behind the main building. The room shared a balcony with the duplex room next door, which was occupied by contract construction workers. They were having a great time firing rifles and pistols right outside our window. It was tough on our one-and-a-half-year-old son, Greg, who had picked up a nasty case of Chicken Pox as we visited fellow missionaries on the journey over.

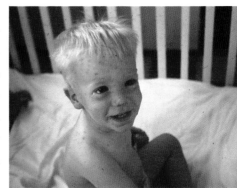

WAR DAMAGE IN NHA TRANG, VIETNAM

About midnight we were sitting in bed and I was writing a letter to Dick Patty in the home office. I told him that the noise was finally beginning to abate.

Then I heard heavy machine gun fire from the perimeter of the U.S. air base close by.

I wondered why, until the rockets and mortars began to land on the base and in town. The noise became deafening – and, honestly, frightening. That, of course, was the launch of the coordinated countrywide Tet Offensive of the Vietcong and North Vietnamese Army. The attack came as close as an MP compound about a block from the Center.

We were not able to go back down to Can Tho to begin our work there. In fact the building the Morgans had suggested for the ministry was badly damaged in the attacks on the town. The sadness of this was increased by the fact that my younger brother was operating out of that area on a boat that delivered special operations troops up the jungle waterways of the Delta. He was not doing well spiritually, and I had really hoped we could be there for him.

The cities and towns of South Vietnam became too dangerous for troops to move around in private activities or to attend the Center, except for those who came by occasionally over the three weeks we were there to give us information. On one occasion they had intel that the Viet Cong were in the neighborhood, and they came with a two-and-a-half ton truck and a gun-jeep to take us to bunkers on Camp McDermott for a night or two.

During this time there was an attack on a missionary group in an upcountry village. Some missionaries were killed and some wounded. The U.S. military evacuated the wounded to the military hospital in Nha Trang, and their family members came to the Center. We were about eighteen souls in the Center for some of the time.

We waited and prayed for the time when we could move on to Can Tho. The time didn't come; and finally Dick got a call through from Denver to ask us to move to Subic Bay temporarily and help the Cadys. I cried. And we obeyed. We never got to return to Vietnam, but as always, in God's wisdom, the time with the Cadys and subsequent time in Thailand became vital parts of our ministry experience.

THAILAND

FRIENDSHIP HOUSE
3957/9 CHAKRI STREET
KORAT, THAILAND
DIRECTORS: DARL AND JAN GOODE

CHRISTIAN SERVICEMEN'S CENTER
100/7 PICHITRUNGSUN ROAD
UBON, THAILAND
DIRECTORS: BILL AND JEANETTE KRAMER

CHRISTIAN SERVICEMEN'S CENTER
693/A BUM ROONG MAUNG
NAKHON PHANOM, THAILAND
DIRECTORS: PAUL AND CAROL KELLEY

SATTAHIB SERVICEMEN'S CENTER
SATTAHIB, THAILAND
DIRECTORS: LOU AND LINDA HARRISON
DARL AND JAN GOODE

THE FRIENDSHIP HOUSE

by Jan Goode, in Remembering God's Faithfulness

This was the rainy season, so even though the days were hot and sticky it cooled down at night and when it rained. That was wonderful. The climate was not as unbearable as I had expected. The sun was very hot, and whenever possible I avoided being out in the heat of the day. I have to admit, I did my share of complaining. One day Scott and I were walking to a store and I commented that the sun was very hot. Scott looked up at me and said, "Mommy did God make the sun?" I got the message!

We looked at quite a few houses before we found "the place" – that large building that would become our home and the Servicemen's Center. We named it Friendship House. We looked at it in the morning and showed it to other missionaries that afternoon. There didn't seem to be any question as to whether we should take it; it seemed so obvious that this was the place. It had been vacant for over a month, and there was no "for rent" sign on it. We thanked the Lord for it. The price was $175 a month, and we rented it on September 22nd. The building was just two blocks away from an ice cream shop, the Foremost Dairy Bar, which was known as the "most place" by the G.I.s in Korat. The structure was concrete and three stories high with a roof garden. Thai kitchens had no built-ins, not even a sink. We chose the room for the kitchen because it had one water faucet. Some basic furniture was included with the building: wardrobes, a glass cupboard, a plastic sofa, and some single beds. The ground floor became the dining room and lounge area. Before we acquired a table and chairs, we managed fine with a piece of crating on top of a frame box and boxes for chairs. The front of the building had two large iron gates. A little later, Darl and some of his helpers replaced them with a double wall and a real door with a round doorknob, just like home. That made a much more attractive entrance and kept out some of the loud street noise and heavy dust.

The cement building was really much cooler than the wooden Thai houses and provided protection from the sun and filth on the streets. It was a great place for Gwen and Scott to play, but there was no yard.

We were excited about finding the building! Darl realized, however, that is was just a tool. He wrote in a letter to Jesse Miller, "I remember our God dwells not in temples made with hands, but in temples of flesh and blood as men make room for Him. That's our big job." We would be ministering to men directly engaged in the Vietnam War. Every morning we were awakened with the noise of bombers taking off, and too often we heard of those who did not return.

Darl and Jan Goode with children Scott, Gwen, and Bruce

FELLOWSHIP AT THE FRIENDSHIP HOUSE

It was the summer of 1968. I traveled back to Korat where I spent most of my ministry days in Thailand with Darl and Jan Goode. They were sure that I hadn't left out one cookie recipe in Jan's cookbook. I insisted on putting nuts in the cookies; however, the only kind we could buy were unroasted Spanish peanuts, which I would bake in the oven and then peel off all the red hulls. Every Sunday afternoon was cookie baking time, with a little help from the military men that were inclined to spend their time in the kitchen. They were to be eaten on Sunday evenings at our OCSC Friendship House weekly fellowships after church service. Nearly everyone came over for a time of fellowship.

Being in Thailand was instrumental in learning many new ways of survival. Theft was something we had to deal with in Korat. The house we lived in was a storefront type building. A number of times it was proven that we could not leave our vehicle on the street. In a few minutes it could be hot wired and driven off, never to be seen again. It was not possible to have a garage, but storefront buildings have large gates through which we drove our car and parked it three feet (that's correct, three feet) away from our dining room table. Many learning experiences come with pioneering a ministry.

When we sat down at a meal, often we would sing before we prayed: "Heaven is better than this, praise God for joy and bliss. I like living for Jesus down here, but heaven is better than this." And then we would grin at one another.

BY LORENE GLYNN

On right: Darl and Jan Goode with Gwen and Scott packing up to move to Thailand.

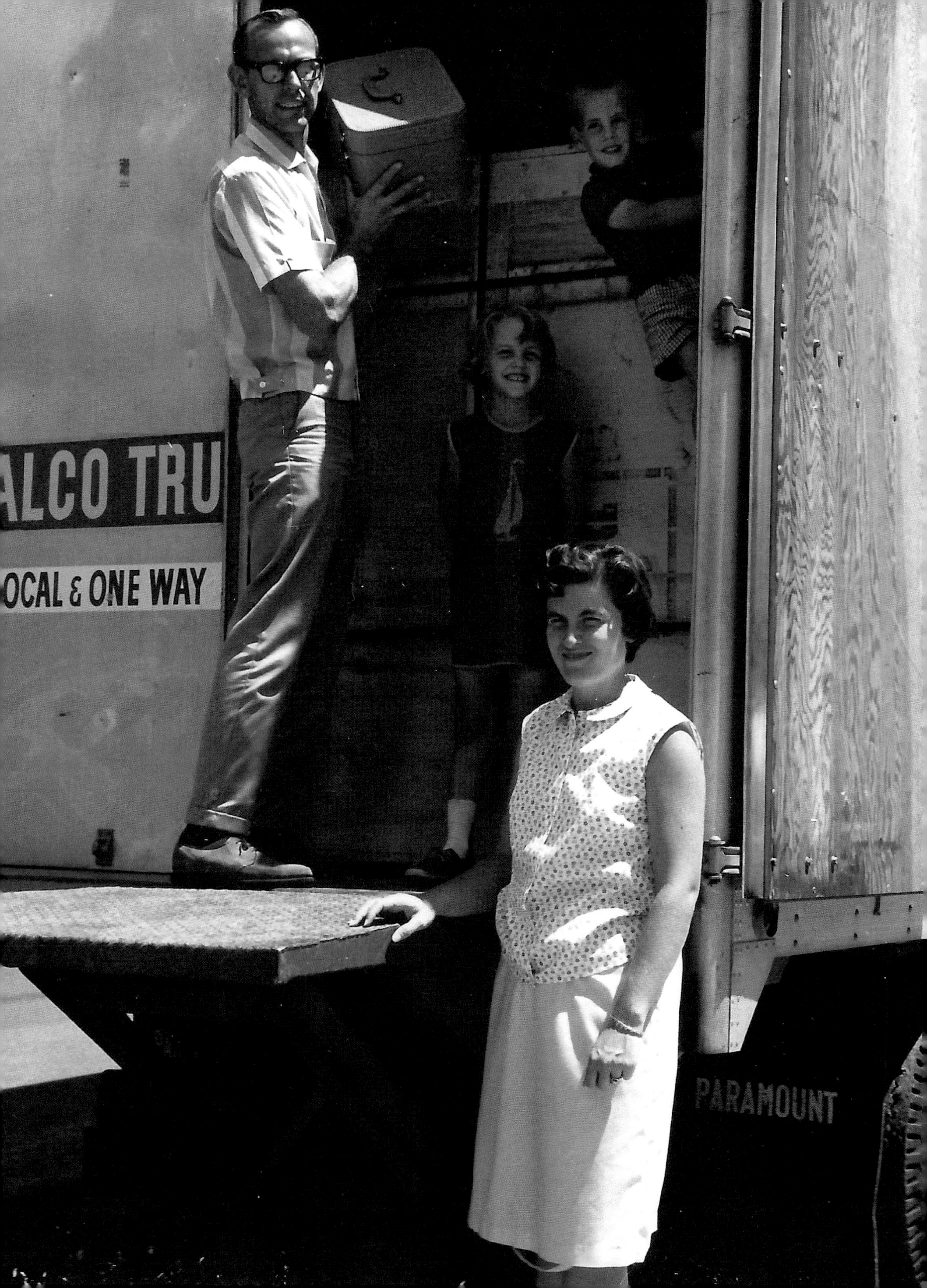

ALCO TRU
OCAL & ONE WAY
PARAMOUNT

PAUL AND CAROL KELLEY WITH CHILDREN JANAE AND ERIC (KYLE LATER JOINED THE FAMILY)

LINDA HARRISON WITH GREG AND ART, JEANNETTE AND BILL KRAMER, SERVICEMEN, AND PAUL KELLEY

UBON, 1968-1974

BILL KRAMER OPENED THE CENTER IN UBON, THAILAND, IN 1968
AND WAS JOINED BY NEW BRIDE, JEANNETTE, IN 1969.

DIRECTED BY GOD

BY BILL KRAMER

"GOD, I DON'T THINK YOU WILL SAVE ME, BUT I WANT TO SERVE YOU."

That was the cry of a 15-year-old who wanted to stop swearing, but couldn't, and it got worse. Confused with life, cursed with swearing, discouraged with being too small to be effective in sports, and failing in academics, how could God ever want me, use me?

I received Christ when I was thirteen or fourteen. I was told to read my Bible and attend church, but nobody told me where to start. In the summer, our youth group would head off to a Christian youth camp. My biggest thrill was to attend all the classes of a missionary from China. I believe that was the beginning of God growing my heart's desire for missions.

In 1951, I joined the navy, still swearing and still trying to find my place in life. God was directing my life, but I didn't know it. I did not like the lifestyle of the other sailors when visiting foreign ports. I wrote to my mother telling her I had no one with whom to go on liberty and I was not about to live like the others. She took my letter into her bedroom and wept, and prayed over it.

After returning to the States, one Saturday night I went to a little Baptist church. I cried out to the Lord, "God, I can't live the Christian life, you've got to live it through me." Sometime during that next week one of the sailors in my shop said, "Kramer, you don't swear anymore, what happened?" God had removed that terrible habit out of my life and I had not realized it. It was about the same time I meet Bill Sawyer who began to teach me how to study the Bible by studying it with me. He taught me how to memorize Scripture by memorizing with me. He taught me how to witness by witnessing with me. Bill and I began to ask God to give us men. Again, He answered our prayers. By the time we were transferred, there were twelve of us studying the Word and praying.

It was during those days when I was growing in the Lord that Pete Peterson and I were on a job. He asked me, "Would God forgive me of my sins if I would ask Him?" As we worked, I shared with Pete some verses on salvation. A week later, he received Christ, and a week after that, his drinking buddy, Jack Watkins, received Christ. Their lives were changed. They stopped bar hopping and started studying the Bible and going on liberty with us.

In 1954, several of us from the ship attended a Navigator Conference in Southern California. The only thing I remember is meeting Dick Patty. That was the beginning of a lifelong friendship.

A couple of years later, I was transferred to a tanker that later pulled into Subic Bay. One night, I was assigned to stand shore patrol in a very unlikely place. It was almost out of town, at the end of a street. God was directing my life. Across the street was a sign leaning against a building that read, "CHRISTIAN SERVICEMEN'S CENTER, WELCOME." The next night I went there and, to my surprise, Dick Patty met me. We were in port over Christmas, so I spent Christmas at the Subic Service Center with Dick and Margaret. The day I left, Dick gave me the verse, "The people who know their God shall be strong and do exploits." (Daniel 11:32b)

In February 1956, I was discharged from the Navy. I was staying at the Long Beach Service Center considering my future when the Lord reminded me of my cry for help when I cried out, "God, I don't think you will save me, but I want to serve you." He had answered the first part. Now I knew I belonged to Him. I knew He had redeemed me. I was His. Now He was reminding me of the second part of my cry, "I want to serve you."

For the next five years, I was involved with the Navigators. I knew I would be a missionary. My heart was in China, but China was not in God's plan for me. During those years, I was burdened for the salvation of my parents. I wanted so much to see them in Heaven and for them to know the same joy that I had. My mother was a godly woman, but my dad, I didn't know. Every time I went home, I tried to talk to him about the Lord, but he would cut me off. He did not want to talk about the Lord, but I so wanted him to know my Jesus.

From 1960 to 1964, I attended Multnomah Bible College. The school was very gracious with me and my academic struggles. During the summer, I worked at Trout Creek Youth Camp. I was encouraged to consider Overseas Christian Servicemen's Centers and believed very strongly that this was where I needed to be. I applied by letter and was turned down. I applied again and was asked to meet the board in Denver. Dick Patty was there and he was the one who had to give me the sad news: I was not accepted.

It was in the fall of 1967, a couple of young men with whom I had served at Trout Creek Youth Camp, had joined the Air Force and returned from a tour of duty in Thailand. I asked them, "Was there any place off base you could go for fellowship?" Their answer was, "No." As I watched them drive away, I said to myself, "Kramer, what are you doing here? You need to be in Thailand."

November 28, my pastor called me into the office. He said, "You had better sit down." I had no idea what was coming. Then he said, "Dick Patty called and O.C.S.C. would like you to be in Thailand by January." That was a month away. I had to get my shots, passport, support, and most importantly, talk to my dear daddy one more time. I was scared. It took courage, but I believed it was God who had ordained it, therefore I accepted.

I traveled to Kansas to be with my parents one more time. My dad was seventy and in poor health. As we returned from a trip to town and pulled into our driveway, I said to my dad, "Daddy, I don't think you're a Christian." His reply, "Well, I guess a guy oughta be." "Would you like to receive Jesus?" "Yes." We prayed. It was like leaving a baby back there when I left. That was the most difficult day of my life. My dad had planned for me to take over the farm, and now there was no one.

By January 1, God had provided all I needed. I believe it was in February I climbed aboard the plane with two other couples, the Harrisons and the Kelleys, and headed for Southeast Asia.

That was forty-seven years ago. God has been, and is still, the conductor of this life that belongs to Him. He continues to answer my prayers. He continues to give me fruit. He is faithful. I love my Lord. I am so grateful for His grace.

STORY OF THREE SOLDIERS

by Lou Harrison

This is a story of God's blessing that is still going on today. It began with a young Christian airman stationed at Utapao Air Base in Thailand attending our Sattahib Servicemen's Center.

Mike *(pictured on the left)* was a quiet, thoughtful guy who loved to tell others about the Lord. He sometimes went alone to the little chicken-coop-like bar street that the Thai and U.S. governments had collaborated to build near the Air Base. They called it "New Land." The shacks in front were bars, and the ones behind housed the girls. Mike walked down the dirt street, visiting the bars and handing out gospel tracts to the soldiers and airmen.

One evening, he gave a tract to a soldier sitting in a bar with a girl on his lap. The soldier, Harry, an Army engineer, tore up the tract. Mike handed him another one. Harry took the girl off his lap and suggested that he and Mike step outside. Mike wondered what this would lead to but was grateful when Harry said, "I was sitting there wondering what would happen if God walked in the place."

Harry soon gave his life to Christ. Mike brought Harry to the Center, and he was making progress in his new walk with the Lord. He began to invite his friend Tim, a bulldozer operator, to the Center. Tim was a smart but cocky guy who enjoyed mocking Harry's new faith. One day he told Harry he would come out to the Center with him. Now Harry panicked, knowing how Tim would likely behave. He actually tried to talk Tim out of coming with him. It didn't work. He came. And sure enough, he practically walked in the door with his mouth running. But God had His hand on Tim's life as he had Harry's. That same evening Tim also gave his heart to Christ.

Tim grew and thrived in his new faith in Christ; and when he rotated back to the U.S. he married a Christian girl and got involved in a local church. Tim and his wife, Maureen, then responded to God's call to serve Him as missionaries, in Thailand, where they have now been serving for more than thirty years — they, and their six kids who are sharing in the ministry with their parents.

LOOKING BACK

A New Sattahib Center

BY LOU HARRISON

God blessed our ministry in Sattahib and kept us busy with airmen and soldiers who were working 7 days a week, 12-hour wartime shifts. So we were sometimes awakened early in the morning with a knock at the gate and the call, "Do you missionaries sleep all day?" by guys who had just finished their night shift. Often I had only returned home at midnight or later after driving dayshift men back to the base.

Yes, the ministry was blessed, but the original center building was small. Though it was located in the closest town, it was 10 kilometers from both the Air Force base and Army post. So God led us to construct a more adequate facility just a couple of kilometers from the air base. This required finding land to lease (by negotiating with the Thai Navy Admiral, as all the land in the area was his bailiwick), finding finances, finding ways of holding down costs, and finding time to do the work while carrying on the current ministry schedule.

Holding the costs down was partly accomplished by God's providing a Chinese Christian building contractor who didn't gouge us. He also took us out for a big dinner in Bangkok as we were departing the country (and I returned to the U.S. with hepatitis). He helped by allowing us to provide the lumber for the job. The Lord put us in contact with the Army officials in charge of demolishing some old buildings on the post. It was good lumber, but lots of work to take the buildings down and keep the wood in good condition. This was wartime, and the military was quite "liberal" with us civilians overseas caring for their soldiers. So when we had lumber to transport to the work site they kindly provided us a two-and-a-half ton truck and driver.

The soldiers and airmen worked their hearts out on this project, using their precious off-duty rest time. They also worked hard at clearing the land (it hurt to have to take down some coconut palms, mango, and papaya trees!), and hand-digging the well with Army trenching tools. The well went 40 ft. deep at one-meter diameter. One of our airmen told me he could get some explosives and dig the well with a shape charge. I said, "Thanks anyway." It sounded too scary. I should have let him do it. When this airman was discharged he built his own successful construction business in North Carolina.

We rotated out of Asia after four-and-a-half years, just before the new center was completed. Darl and Jan Goode relieved us, finished the building, and used it until the U.S. vacated the bases in Thailand. We had the opportunity to visit the building, now occupied by business people, in 1989 during our Asia-Pacific staff conference in Pattaya Beach.

Dick Patty, General Director of O.C.S.C., visiting the Harrisons in Sattahib.

Dick Patty with Art, Lou, Linda, and Greg Harrison (Christina later joined the family)

Greg Harrison evangelizing with Thai children that always gathered around him and Art when the family walked down to the beach.

Linda crossing the Mekong River with missionary friends into Cambodia for visa renewal.

Linda Harrison with Greg and Art on a visa renewal trip.

20 YEARS AT SUBIC

BY CYRIL (DAD) BROOKS

Some 200 years ago the English poet William Cowper wrote:

"God moves in a mysterious way, His wonders to perform;
He plants His footsteps in the sea, and rides upon the storm.
Deep in unfathomable mines of never-failing skill,
He treasures up His bright designs, and works His sovereign will."

It is only as we look back over the years that we are able to see how God has been working out His sovereign will, though to God it was all plain from the beginning.

The story of Overseas Christian Servicemen's Centers really goes back to a time before World War II, when a young eighteen-year-old airman went to meetings in a missionary's home in the suburbs of Manila. There, Jesse Miller learned from keen servicemen that the Bible is more than a book to read in church. His Christian life took on new meaning as God prepared him for the rugged days ahead. *There he decided that his home, if ever he had one, would be open to servicemen.*

Transferred from Nichols Field to Clark a few months before the outbreak of the Pacific War, Jesse survived the vicious bombing of Clark by the Japanese the first day of war. Then came retreat to the hills and horrors of Bataan, three months of disease and starvation, then defeat and surrender in April 1942, the terrible death-march from Bataan to Tarlac and prison camp there.

One day, Jesse faced a Japanese firing squad because one of their group had left for the hills. God moved in a mysterious way when He asked Jesse just then, "Are you willing to come back here as a missionary?" The
unseen response was "Yes, Lord." The seen results were the Japanese saying, "Tomorrow" – a tomorrow that never came, instead was a transfer to Japan and three years of hard work as a prisoner of war.

Then release, return to home and loved ones. Jesse Miller went to Bible school in California, then returned to the Philippines with the Far Eastern Gospel Crusade – an answer to his promise to the Lord in prison camp. Soon after, he married a beautiful tall blonde, a missionary in Japan and brought her to this country. One day the mission received a request for someone to act as auxiliary chaplain at the Air Force depot in Manila. That assignment was given to Jesse and again we see God working "His wonders to perform." That service led to the conversion of several men over a period of months, some of which are now serving with O.C.S.C. – Carroll Tarkington, Tom Hash and Chuck Hall. Soon there were contacts at Sangley naval base. Some of us remember those fast trips across Manila Bay, often drenched with spray. A later contact from Sangley was Ben Cady, now with O.C.S.C. at Misawa, Japan.

Typhoon rains were pouring down one day as I was doing some carpentry work in my home. The Millers arrived, excited about a new home that could be rented. They wanted us to see it, in the rain! It proved very suitable and that's where Dick and Margaret Patty were married twenty years ago.

Dick Patty was burdened for the need at this great navy base in Subic. Reaching the Philippines in February 1955, the first center was opened here in June of that year. In October 1955, Margaret Olsen worked her way on a ship coming to the Philippines and on October 31st was married to Dick Patty. In the absence of her parents it was my great privilege to give away the bride.

Much of Olongapo near the main gate was then swamp land being filled and reclaimed. O.C.S.C. was granted a permit by the US Navy to build on this present location. Ray Kalbach, who was an industrial arts teacher in a Christian high school in Manila, was able to help in the building program. With his humor, this was "Olonga-pew" and jeepneys were "unguided missiles." Much money, work, and effort went into the planning and building of this functional center – Dick put more into it than he intended when he sliced off part of this thumb. The building was put into use in December 1961, though it took a couple more years to finish it.

The accomplishments of this place are not to be seen in the facilities freely provided; not in the number of meals served nor the count of overnight guests; not even in the ministry of the book room or tape library. The real accomplishment of this home has been in the lives of men and women changed, transformed by the power of God. Only God knows how many men have been snatched from the pits of corruption and the snares of sin. In this home, their faces and lives have been turned toward God.

During the past 20 years several people have been building upon the foundation laid by Dick and Margaret Patty. Ray and Alice Kalbach had a share in building lives as well as building the center. There comes to mind (I hope I don't forget any) Bob and Dorothy Bingham, Sid Hendry, Tom and Dotty Hash, Miss Lorene Glynn, Ben and Connie Cady, Ralph and Wilma Porter, Abe and Ellen Teeny, Lou and Linda Harrison, Jim and Betty Hendricks, John and Joan Hobson, Ralph and Betty Camp, Roy and Bettie Jordan, and now of course, Jerry and Irene Bates with Udell and Janet Meyers.

We gather today in this beautiful center with its excellent facilities. Let us never forget this all came about through the faithfulness of God in supplying the needs of this work through these 20 years. There has been a consistent reliance upon God, not upon endowments, wealthy foundations nor even support of any denomination. God has supplied the needs through the sacrificial gifts of His people, praying friends in America, and also by many men and women who have been blessed by God here in this Subic Servicemen's Center.

Only when we stand in God's presence in glory will we fully know all that God has done in these 20 years at Subic. Cowper had another stanza in that poem which I started:

"His purposes will ripen fast, unfolding every hour.
The bud may have a bitter taste but sweet will be the flower."

There have been bitter moments, times of trial and testing and these will continue as long as we are down here. Today we see something of the sweetness and fragrance of the flower that has budded here. We confidently await the day of Christ at His return when all His purposes for this work will have blossomed and have been revealed.

THE MOST IMPORTANT PRAYER
REQUEST TO GIVE YOURSELF UNTO IS
FOR THE YOUNG, TENDER CHILDREN
OF GOD WHO ARE DAILY BEING FOUND
IN THE RANKS OF THE U.S. MILITARY
FORCES. PRAY THAT GOD WILL GIVE
THEM THE NEEDED STRENGTH TO BE
GOOD SOLDIERS OF JESUS CHRIST.

Tom Hash

LIVES
CHANGED

by Jesse Miller

Many stories could be shared regarding the faithfulness of God
to us. The greatest miracles have been those whose lives have been
changed! Lives of men and women who were headed in the wrong direction, turned around and made God their goal. Lives so bent and broken by
sin, brought to a personal relationship with the One who heals the broken
in heart. Lives so weak as to be most often "in the slough of despond,"
transformed by dependence on the power of the Holy Spirit into a life
that flows over with the goodness and grace of God. Lives so religious
but ineffective to help another, changed into loving and helping
others come to know Christ. Lives of those who never hun-
gered for the Word of God but called themselves Christians, changed into men and women of the Word.
These are the truly eternal miracles we
witnessed.

JESSE, SID, TARK, AND DICK IN COLORADO IN 1968

HARRIET REHNKE FAITHFULLY SERVED AT THE HOME OFFICE
FOR 37 YEARS.

WHAT GOD WOULD DO

"I HAVE BEEN YOUNG, AND NOW AM OLD, YET I HAVE NOT SEEN THE RIGHTEOUS FORSAKEN."

PSALM 37:25

Before Tom and I even knew each other, both of us had a sense of God's call to serve Him as missionaries, and later the Lord in His Word gave me clear direction to serve with OCSC. When the going got really tough during our first term of ministry in Panama, we knew in our hearts that we were in the very center of His will even though we were being attacked on every side almost to the point of despair. In retrospect, we know that God was taking us through the refining process: boiling away the dross, skimming off the waste, seeking the fine, pure gold that reflected His likeness. Was it painful? You bet! Was it worth it? Oh yes!

Some of you can relate. Those of you who are new in your journey of faith and ministry, have yet to endure the refining fire. But it will come! Determine before the Lord to suffer well. We went to Panama eager to serve the Lord and see many soldiers come to know Him. Not a bad motive, really! But God had a better one – not what we could do for Him, but what He would do in us. He was testing our faith, and if we responded well we would have the privilege of serving Him for many years of fruitful ministry to come. And that is exactly what happened.

DOTTY HASH, *IN HER EIGHTIES LOOKING BACK*

A NEW DECADE

BY DICK PATTY, GENERAL DIRECTOR OF O.C.S.C. 1967-1978
TO O.C.S.C. MISSIONARIES IN THE CENTER CIRCUIT PUBLICATION
DECEMBER 31, 1969

Tonight at midnight we enter a new decade. The '60s are over – history. Important years they were! Only eternity will display all that God has done in the hearts of servicemen and their families during these years through your ministry.

Our usefulness to the Lord will largely stem from our comprehension of and faithfulness to His changeless character and purposes. At the same time our effectiveness as individuals and as an organization ministering to servicemen of this generation will depend a great deal on our ability to cope with change. We must with perception and diligence sort out that which is Christian from that which is cultural, that which is eternal from that which is temporal. They properly occupy much of our time and energy and are intricately woven into most every phase of our ministry. But having distinguished them from the absolutes we allow them to – yes, even cause them to – change.

The human heart craves for surroundings that are stable and circumstances that are both friendly and predictable. We cherish every partial realization of this ambition, but must steady our hearts in the conviction that fulfillment awaits us in heaven. We are pilgrims here.

OUR TIME FOR COURAGE & FAITH

BY DAVID SCHROEDER, PRESIDENT OF CADENCE INTERNATIONAL, 1995 – PRESENT
JUNE 3, 2015

I can almost hear the clock ticking like a metronome in the background. Dick Patty hunches over a typewriter – with furrowed brow he formulates words to encourage the OCSC team as the mission pivots into the new decade of the 1970's. And what wonderful and timeless words these were – words that transcend generations, bridge decades, and connect history, present, and future.

As in 1969, so today we must be focused on knowing and loving God's "changeless character and purposes." Only God remains the same. He is our only rock and strong tower. We must with "perception and diligence sort out that which is Christian from that which is cultural." Every generation must seek God's wisdom in discerning the truth from the lies – the Christian from the cultural. Many of the cultural challenges remain the same; some that we face today, our mission founders could never have imagined.

And yes, perhaps most importantly, we must sort out "that which is eternal from that which is temporal." Even as we continue to provide loving and powerful environments in our homes and ministries that are "both friendly and predictable," we must also "steady our hearts in the conviction that fulfillment awaits us in heaven."

The clock continues its faithful, metronomic ticking.

I was seven years old when Dick typed these timeless truths in 1969 and OCSC had only existed for fifteen years! Presently, well, we are all much older – the hours, days, and years have marched relentlessly on. I'm writing these words today on a laptop seated in a chair in my Colorado living room. As it happens, I can see Dick Patty through the window – he's hunched over again, now on his hands and knees working in our backyard garden. He is 89 years old, and he is working that soil with the same thoughtful care with which he also crafted his words for all these years. This man is not just a Cadence founder and pillar to me; he is my father-in-law, mentor, and friend. Not just his words inspire me, but his long-term faithfulness to Jesus moves me to tears and stirs me to that same high standard and calling.

Friends, let us all live up to the legacy and calling passed on to us by this amazing and faithful generation. We are entrusted with today's passing minutes to live and share this precious gospel. The clock is still ticking, and so I leave you now with Dick Patty's words in 1969:

We are pilgrims here.

EPILOGUE

Joyce Schroeder

The pages in the history of Cadence continue to turn. Many more brave and hard-working missionaries have left home and family to answer God's call to minister to the military around the world. A vast army of prayer warriors and sacrificial supporters have partnered in this work. Many ministries have been pioneered – to military youth, women, children, and to militaries of other nations. Cadence missionaries have left Cadence to begin new mission organizations. Military personnel and dependents whose lives were transformed by Christ have gone on to raise godly families, serve their country, and become leaders in their churches and communities.

As we have gathered the stories you have just read, we are very aware, as Lou Harrison puts it, that these are "a few pictures and stories out of some of the most intense, confusing, frightening, sometimes painful, and sometimes fruitful years of our lives."

And so we say "thank you" to all who are part of the ongoing Cadence story. We give glory to God, for *"it was not by their sword that they won the land, nor did their arm bring them victory; it was your right hand, your arm, and the light of your face, for you loved them"* (Psalm 44:3). We honor those who have gone before in the journey of obedience to Christ no matter how "confusing, frightening, sometimes painful, and sometimes fruitful" the path. And we celebrate these real-deal people of faith who laid the good foundation of Cadence International, and who continued to walk with God all the days of their lives.

Now let us go forward and follow their example. Let us be courageous men and women of faith. Let us fix our eyes on Jesus.

"Therefore, since we have so great a cloud of witnesses surrounding us, let us also lay aside every encumbrance and the sin which so easily entangles us, and let us run with endurance the race that is set before us, fixing our eyes on Jesus, the author and perfecter of faith" (Hebrews 12:1-2).

facing page: Bill Kramer preparing to go overseas

SERVICEMEN'S BIBLE CONFERENCE
DANIEL PURPOSED IN HIS HEART JUNE '66

through the years

O.C.S.C./CADENCE MISSIONARIES

Harland & Frances Abbott

Tad & Cindy Aldrich

Bob & Karen Alston

Anthony & Jessica Amor

Robert & Clarice Anderson

Cathy Anderson

Adam Anderson

Pete & Dorothy Anderson

Eric & Teresa Anderson

Ron & Sunny Anderson

Ryan Anderson

Steve & Pam Andrews

Bill & Sue Angliss

Matthew & Sarah Annanie

Douglas & Peggy Arendsee

Drew & Shelly Arliskas

Sondra Armstrong

Leonard & Elizabeth Arnold

Jack & Virginia Ashcraft

Greg & Teri Atkinson

Tyson & Caralee Aufdenberg

Wes & Elaine Auldridge

Dave & Beth Babb

Matthew & Jill Bachali

Steve Bailey

Don & Nancy Baker

Brad & Dee Ball

David & Janice Barbour

Diana Bartz

Jerry & Irene Bates

Stan & Ellen Beach

Todd & Penny Beaudin

Earl & Barbara Beegle

Jim & Angel Benge

Jeffrey & Lori Bennett

Bob & Dusty Bennett

Larry & Evelyn Bentley

Tim & Bobbi Bettger

Deedra Bingham

Bob & Dorothy Bingham

Ed & Joy Bissonnette

Larry & Brender Blakely

Dave & Mary Blatchford

Steve & Kristy Blehm

Ben & Melody Bloker

Ron & Marlene Blough

Dave & Jean Bobbey

Jerry & Katherine Boland

Randy Bonser

James & Martha Bowden

Aaron Box

James & Virginia Boyle

Bernie & Gail Boyne

Paul & Sandra Bradley

Billy & Stacey Brand

Frank & Ruth Ann Branham

Anna Bresko

Brenda Brewer

Becky Briggs

Dale & Marian Brock

Sharane Brockmeyer

Dick & Joan Brown

Wilfried & Lydia Bruns

Milt & Jeannie Bryan

Stephanie Bucklew

Doug & Sarah Bunger

Ryan & Amy Burglehaus

Ed & Suzie Buri

Ben & Connie Cady

Ralph & Betty Camp

Jeff & Candy Campbell

Susan Campbell

Tony & Susan Capelli

Jeff & Sue Carlson

Greg & Heidi Carlson

Melissa Carnegie

Paul & Stacy Cassidy

Bob & Stephanie Caudle

Uk & Manuela Chong

Bryan & Suzanne Chrisman

Nikki Cline

Nadine Coates

Bernie & Bea Coffin

Bernie & Fran Coffin

Christopher Cohoon

Jim & Sarah Collison

Dan & Laura Combes

Ken & Julie Converse

Phil & Donna Cook

David Cordell

Jose & Whitney Cordero

Eric & Barbara Cox

Richie Cox

Susan Coyle

Tony & Chris Curtisi

Ward & Margaret Cushman

Danielle Cutter

Walt & Delcy Davenport

George & Lillian Davis

Mel & Patty Davis

Brian & Lori Davis

Shari Davis

David DeJong

Tom & Audrey De Rivera

Grover & Nancy De Vault

John & Debbie DeLuca

Mark & Linda DeYmaz

Ron & Liz Dice

Lynn & Judy Doty

Harley & Miriam Dow

Bruce & Wendy Dower

Sareth Duaong

Russ & Kristen Eddleman

James & Mary Egeland

Terry & Lori Einfalt

Brad & Debbie Ellgen

Richard & Pamela
 Ellgen

Ernie & Bobbie Elmore

Anessa Erickson

Chuck & Naom Estey

Dan & Barb Evans

Keith & Ruth Ann Farmer

Jeff & Jeaneen Fields

Mark & Mary Fischer

Steven & Kathleen Fisher

Gwen Fitzgerald

Benny Flores

Gerry & Ellen Fox

Barb France

Darrow & Vicki Frazier

Pat Friedline

Kenji & Amy Fukunaga

Larry & Karen Gaither

Brown & Ginger Gaulden

Alex & Denise Ghioni

Bruce & Cathy Gilbert

Laurel Givry

Lorene Glynn

Darl & Janice Goode

George & Kay Goolde

Jonathan & Christine
 Graham

Megan Gray

Gary & Cheryl Greene

Lanny & Stacey Groves

Gordon & June Gustafson

Daniel & Becke Haas

Andrea Haddock

Rebekah Hager

Wayne & Melody Hala

Chuck & Jane Hall

Chuck & Janice Hall

Robert & Karen Hampton

Ron & Susan Hand

Kim Haneline

Michele Hanson

Lou & Linda Harrison

Steven & Rachel Harvell

Tom & Sarah Harvey

Tom & Dotty Hash

Dan & Laura Hash

Ray & Char Hauser

Tim & Rebecca Hawkins

Bill & Cindy Haynes

Jim & Betty Hendricks

Sid & Annette Hendry

Holly Hentschel

Margarite Hill

Sandi Hiller

Kalob & Chelse Hinners

John & Joan Hobson

Obe & Mary Ann Hokanson

Sharyn Holl

Robert & Ruth Ann
   Holthouse

Frank & Eloise Hooper

Janet Hooper

Harry & Doreen Horn

Brad & Cheryl Hostetler

Jim & Nancy Howard

Joe & Desiree Hudson

Matt & Tina Huisjen

Warren & Peggy Hume

Brian & Cathy Hutchens

David & Andrea Hutchings

Ben & Doris Hyde

Larry & Linda Ingalls

Alex & Isabel Jaruchik

Bradley & Laurel Jenkins

Craig & Kim Jentink

Andrew & Anna Johnson

Nate & Louise Johnson

Chris & Jenny Jolin

Roy & Bettie Jordan

Ray & Alice Kalbach

Neva Kasen

Jay & Jerri Kayll

Paul & Carol Kelley

Mark & Kerry Kellond

Rich & Jean Kerr

Sarah Kidd

Roland Kincher

Bruce & Darlene Kinde

Peter & Tanya Kinney

Brian & Aimee Kleager

Wendy Kline

Bernie & Anne Koch

Mary Koedyker

Mark & Carol Kohl

Jan Kohlmann

Homer & Dee Kohn

Bill & Jeannette Kramer

Bill & Kathy Ladd

Jan Lahman

Del & Jeanne Laitinen

David & Bonnie Lambert

Katie Lambert

Jennifer Larsen

Nick & Rebecca Laurenzana

Juliana Law

Thomas & Yvette
   Leightenheimer

Nina Leonard

Albert & Pilo Letting

Ardith Libby

Erik & Jennifer Liebenthal

Jimmy & Kendra Limneos

Heather Lite

Heidi Long

Kenny & Joy Lowe

Edward & Helen Luckey

Mark & Sonya Lybarger

Beth Mabry

Carl & Joyce Main

Skip & Ruth Main

Marla Mancini

Richard & Nona Marshall

Mike Martin

Harold & Edna Matolka

Steve & Teeter Mauldin

Christopher & Elizabeth May

Judy McCarthy

Rebecca McClure

Clair & Joan McCombs

Dan McCord

Kyle Mellander

Ed & Carmen Merritt

Dave & Betty Meschke

Jim & Deby Meschke

Paul & Beryl Metko

Erv & Elsie Meyer

Udell & Janet
   Meyers

Jim & Alice Mikos

Bob & Annie Miller

Jesse & Nettie Miller

Jim & Lina Miller

Gaynor & Barbara Moline

Mark & Joyce Monsees

Lem & Marge Morgan

Scotty & Sue Morrison

Brian & Christina Mulder

Bob Murphy

Chuck & Kathy Myer

Sandy & Sue Nafziger

TOP LEFT: CHAPLAIN DAVE MESCHKE ON THE LEFT
TOP RIGHT: JIM AND BETTY HENDRICKS
BOTTOM LEFT: C.P. TARKINGTON
BOTTOM RIGHT: MARGARET AND JOYCE PATTY, CHRISTMAS 1963

Vince & Nancy Nash

Lynette Nelson

Marlys Newey

Roger & Sheila Nielson

Gary & Ru Nitta

Carla Ogden

David Olander

Dennis & Betty Ortman

Mark & Jennifer Oshman

Daniel Palmberg

Alicia Parsons

Sharlene Patrick

Dick & Margaret Patty

Josh & Kristi Patty

Dave & Connie Patty

Steve Patty

Mike & Rachel Paulson

David & Mo Pavelec

Chris & Bekah Pawlowski

Michael & Jonna Payne

Martha Pearson

Grady & Ali Pennell

Danny & Kathryn Perez

Mel & Darlene Pike

Ken & Andrea Pitcher

Kevin & Michelle Pollock

Ed & Carol Pomelear

Gene & Anne Poppino

Bill Porter

Ralph & Wilma Porter

David & Melanie Powell

Jeremy & Shawna
    Quattlebaum

Melissa Rafferty

Donald & Patricia Raker

Jennessa Randall

Buddy & Jennifer Rathmell

Julie Rathmell

John & Alma Ray

Don & Linda Reasoner

Johnathan & Stephenie Reilly

Carl Reinhardt

Pete & Anastasia Remmes

Dick & MaryEtta Reynolds

Doug & Heike Riddle

Paul Riess

David & Dianne Roberts

Ron & Vicky Rogers

Al & Marilyn Romaneski

Harry & Marion Ross

Dennis & Jeannie Roth

Lou & Cathy Rozmiarek

Dawn Rubottom

Chuck & Susan Ruge

Grant & Norma Russell

Tony & Melody Sandoval

James & Kathleen Sands

Bill & Sylvia Sawyer

Allison Schaffner

Kevin & Sharon Scheible

Michael & Andrea
    Schellenberg

Ray & Jan Schmautz

Buddy & Evelyn Schofield

Kat Schoggen

David & Joyce Schroeder

Matt & Ruth Schroeder

Rick & Paula Scott

Jim & Denise Scott

Jeff & Julie Shackelford

Chris & Julie Sharber

David & Jeanni Shepherd

Ed & Amber Shipp

Rich & Melissa Short

Don & Michelle Shove

Bill & Connie Shryock

Greg & Kathy
  Siegfriedt-Wilson

Carol Simning

Bob & Cindy Skinner

Diana Smith

Joel Smith

Sharlene Smith

Curt & Sharon Snell

Deric & Rebecca Sneller

Daryl & June Soey

Jeffrey & Brigetta Somerville

Doyle & Chris Spader

Stephen & Anna Stager

Chet Steffey

Al & Jeanie Stirling

Fred & Diane Stock

Kelly Strope

C.P. & Alma Tarkington

Beth Tarkington

Clyde & Jane Taylor

Doug & Willi Taylor

Rod Taylor

Abe & Ellen Teeny

Eric & Janet Thimell

Randy Thompson

Todd & Karla Tillapaugh

Jeremy & Lindsey Todd

Pat Tomlingson

Angie Tucker

Jim & Rachel Turnage

Trudy Underwood

Richard & Janice Utecht

Leah Vanderlaan

Phil & Lois Waggoner

Bruce & Teresa Wareing

Don & Jean-Marie Weber

Ron & Pam Weinzapfel

Keith & Anne Wheeler

Bruce & Linda White

Chris Williams

Hugh & Debbie Wilson

Ron & Belle Wilson

Mark & Kathy Wilson

Jim & Diane Wilson

Rebekah Wininger

Don & Lana Jo Winn

Roger & Barbara Wisdom

Dave & Robin Wisner

Jason & Cindy Wolden

Jill Wolfe

Cliff & Edith Woods

Larry & Lois Woodward

Ken & Judi Wooten

Kevin Yapp

HEADQUARTER EMPLOYEES

Naomi Abdilla
Steven Adams
Judy Anderson
Connie Banks
Diana Bartz
Marlina Bello
Cindy Berner
Ginny Black
Cuc Kim Blessitt
Deirdre Brouer
Lisa Butts
Synthea Bystrzycki
Laura Callison
Kirk Cutler
David DeJong
Michael Endres
Sylvia Erickson
Megan Evans

Kimberly Gilman
Christine Graham
Natalie Harper
Rachael Hartman
Debbie Headrick
Tavia Heckle
Lynn Heidebrecht
Shannon Howland
Liz Jackson
Alicia Kliewer
Joel Koedyker
Bonnie Lambert
JoAnn Larrabee
Joanne Lavin
Casey LeTellier
Stacy Ludwig
Carol Mathers
Trisha McCarty-Luedke

Helen Merilatt
Bethany Miles
John Miller
Jeng Mitchell
Jamie Morton
Kim Mouty
Samuel Ndegwa
Dayton Nelson
Barbara Ohno
Darin Pearson
Cassandra Pence
Karol Ruff
Kyle Quiroz
Harriet Rehnke
Emily Rinard
April Robbins
Mara Sakry
Kerith Schroeder

Kyrie Schroeder
Carissa Sheehan
Ainessa Shiffer
Angie Sprague
Tracy Spitler
Donna Stout
Inga Swope
Jami Tauer
Robert Taylor
Donna Tolly
Dave VanValkenburg
Brian Warren
Anna Warren
Rex West
Stacy Wiens
Theresa Wilson
Ann White
Ryan Zeiset

BOARD OF DIRECTORS

listed chronologically

Jesse Miller
Dick Patty
C.P. Tarkington
Tom Hash
Sid Hendry
David Meschke
Wendell Grout
James Maxson
Willard Taussig
Robert Benson
John Stevens
Keith Williams
Ray Buker
Gordon Gustafson
Ben Cady
Leslie Goodman
William Sandven

Ted Klingsmith
Paul Pettijohn
Russell Honeywell
John Roberts
Joel Stoen
Bill Boyd
Stan Noreen
David Solver
Don Orvis
Bob Heavner
Bob Bingham
Harold Carlson
Wayne Hala
Abe Teeny
Lem Morgan
Frank Tillapaugh
Ron Gallagher

Glenn Mohr
Norm Magnus
Jack Dawson
Bud Peterson
Stacy Bragg
Rob Woodruff
Jim Olson
Jack McCullough
Liam Atchison
Terry Anderson
Dave Farr
Joel Wall
Keita Andrews
Richard Newman
David Schroeder
Jim Howard
Todd Cienski

Jeff Easley
Curtis Kemp
Jerri Kayll
Betty Price
Alan Villanueva
Rick Garris
Frank Oakley
Steve Castlen
Cindy Zulli
John Albers
Ron Welch
Patricia Cole
Thom Scheffel
Claudia Ingram
Drew Arliskas

(L-R) SID HENDRY, DICK PATTY, TOM HASH, DAVE MESCHKE, LOU HARRISON, C.P. TARKINGTON IN 1994

JESSE AND NETTIE MILLER

C.P. AND ALMA TARKINGTON

TOM AND DOTTY HASH

DICK AND MARGARET PATTY

ACKNOWLEDGEMENTS

Joyce Schroeder – Editor
www.cadence.org

Lauren Reavely – Designer
www.laurenreavely.com

Stacy Wiens – Original Vision for this book
Director of Communications for Cadence International

Article authors and publications noted throughout

Books cited:

Prisoner of Hope by Jesse L. Miller
Copyright 1988, 1989, 1996
Pages: 24, 72-76, 158-159, 171, 183

Fill These Rooms by Dorothy M. Hash
Copyright 1998
Pages: 79, 94-96, 143-145, 153, 156-158

Remembering God's Faithfulness by Janice Goode
Copyright 2009
Pages: 45-46, 67-68, 82-84

CADENCE
PRESS

ISBN: 9780692466384

Printed in USA

Made in the USA
Charleston, SC
16 December 2015